The
Home-Based Bookstore

Start Your Own Business Selling Used Books on Amazon, eBay or Your Own Web Site

Weber Books

Falls Church, VA

www.WeberBooks.com

Steve Weber

WITHDRAWN

The
Home-Based Bookstore

Start Your Own Business Selling Used Books on Amazon, eBay or Your Own Web Site

By Steve Weber

Published by Stephen W. Weber
Printed in the United States of America
Weber Books   www.WeberBooks.com

Author: Steve Weber
Editor: Jill Hacker
Copy editor: Michael McIrvin
Cover design: Brion Sausser
ISBN: 0977240606
Library of Congress Control Number: 2005936115

Contents

Warning and Disclaimer

This book describes the author's experiences selling used books online. It is offered with the understanding that it does not contain legal, financial, or other professional advice. Individuals requiring such services should consult a competent professional.

Although every effort has been made to ensure the accuracy of the contents of this book, errors and omissions may occur. The publisher assumes no responsibility for any damages arising from the use of this book, or alleged to have resulted in connection with this book.

This book is not completely comprehensive. Some readers may wish to consult additional books and advice before making decisions about establishing a business or changing their current business practices. Additional sources of information are identified in the appendices of this book.

Why Online Bookselling?

Selling used books on the Internet is one of the greatest opportunities available to small entrepreneurs today. Used book sales on the Internet jumped 33 percent in 2004. Now, one of every 12 books sold is a used book, and two-thirds of those are purchased online from small businesses — with total annual sales of $609 million.

You can be part of this expanding market. For less than $100, you can launch an Internet bookselling business with profit margins rivaling those of any business. Exactly how much money you earn depends mostly on how much effort you put into your new enterprise.

If you're already employed, you can begin your book business as a part-time venture, as I did five years ago. If the profits from bookselling grow bigger than your paycheck (it took three months for me), you can quit your job and enjoy one of the most rewarding experiences of your life: building a thriving business from scratch.

Nothing is more empowering than building your own business to support yourself and your family, and perhaps no line of work is more highly regarded than bookselling. Sellers of used books help build a better world by preserving and spreading knowledge. The used-book trade helps our communities by conserving resources, reducing the waste going to landfills, and making books more affordable.

You don't need a store or a warehouse or delivery trucks to sell used books. You don't need an MBA or inside connections with wholesalers or drop-shippers. You needn't be an expert on books, though a fondness for books will surely help. The only requirements are a willingness to learn and a commitment to running an honest business.

You can start small – with the books on your own shelf — and you can invest your profits in new inventory and expand at your own pace. No business is better suited for the one-person company than used bookselling. If you'd like to earn just a few hundred dollars a month to supplement your current income, you can keep the enterprise a part-time job. If you want to take four months off during the year, you can. If you want to go full-time, it's certainly possible to earn more than $40,000 a year working on your own.

I started selling books on the Internet in 2001 after discovering the Web site Half.com. I listed a couple dozen of my unwanted books for sale and was amazed to see how quickly they sold. I couldn't wait to find new books to list. Impulsively, I withdrew $80 from my meager savings to buy four bags of used paperbacks from a local shop. Several of the books turned out to be worthless, but one book sold immediately for $23, and within a few days, I had doubled my $80 investment after selling just half of those books. I was hooked.

That weekend, I hauled a carload of books home from a library sale and worked straight through the weekend listing them on the Internet. I quit my job two months later and never looked back. In the meantime, I've sold books worth a total of $1 million to 80,000 customers in all 50 states and 31 foreign countries. With the profits I've paid off my debts and moved from a cramped one-bedroom apartment to a nice house. And all of it came from the $80 I spent on that first batch of books and the urge to see what was possible.

All this was impossible a few years ago. To be a used bookseller before recent innovations, you had to first assemble 10,000 to 20,000 books. You needed to lease retail space. You needed employees. You had to pay through the nose to advertise, and then you would pray some customers showed up with money in hand. If something went sufficiently wrong, you lost your shirt.

Today, you can market instantly to a worldwide pool of millions of ready buyers — even as a beginning used bookseller. You don't need to advertise, and participating in this growing network costs you nothing until you make your sales.

Used books are the perfect merchandise to sell online for several reasons:

- Books are easy to find at low cost.
- Books are standardized items that are simple to describe and sell.
- Books are compact, non-fragile, and easy to ship.
- Most used books are worth less than $20, and so bookselling attracts few of the thieves and scam artists that plague most online ventures.

This is an excellent time to get into online book-selling too. Every day new buyers are discovering they can get a used book at a great price online. People who never thought of buying a used book before are discovering the great value, convenience, and selection available through online sellers. Buyers can choose from more than 2.5 million unique titles online, compared to 20,000 books at an average mall bookstore.

I can't guarantee you'll make money selling used books. Most booksellers don't get rich, and quite a few go broke. This is not a get-rich-quick scheme. It's hard work. But it's a lot easier to work hard at your own business than for someone else — you reap the rewards.

Assuming you don't make the mistake of opening a walk-in store or hiring employees, you can keep your risk very close to zero. Following the suggestions in this book, you should be able to buy plenty of books for a dollar or two each and sell most of them for $8 to $10. It's hard to lose money with profit margins like that.

When I started, I knew nothing about selling books, but it's amazing how fast you can learn by doing something you enjoy. A few people tried to talk me out of writing what you hold in your hands right now, saying I should keep what I've learned to myself. "Don't help your competition," they warned. But I don't look at it that way. Since you're reading this book, you're either interested in selling books or may have already started. The ideas in this book will help you take your business to the next level faster than you can through trial and error. And if you run a good bookselling operation, that helps me — if you make a buyer happy, maybe they'll buy from me next time. That buyer will tell their friends about getting used books online, and so on.

My theory about selling used books online is that everyone can win. The more people who become buyers and sellers in this worldwide network, the more valuable it is for everyone to belong. Buyers can find more of what they want, and sellers have more buyers every day.

You might not agree with everything in this book, however. Perhaps after reading this, you'll come up with some better ideas. If you do, or if you think I've got something wrong or left something out, I'd enjoy hearing from you.

Write to me at feedback@weberbooks.com.

-- All the best,
Steve Weber

Where to Find Books

To find books that can be resold profitably, you'll need to find sources in your area where you can select from a large number of used books at low prices. Later, we'll discuss exactly which books to pick, but for now, let's consider where you'll have the best chance of finding them. After a while, you'll discover which places are best, and make those part of your regular rounds. Here's where to start:

Library sales. In most areas, library sales are by far the best source of stock for booksellers. Sales are often conducted monthly, usually on a Saturday, and feature a wide variety of books at very low prices.

Most library sales are organized by a nonprofit Friends of the Library (FOL) group, and most of the books for sale are donated by area residents in very good or like-new condition. Because the library can't absorb most of this material into its collection, the surplus is offered for public sale as a fundraiser. Nearly all the books are priced at a dollar or two apiece, and again, lots of them can be sold for $10 or more online.

Sellers who have learned what books to look for can come away from a good-sized library sale with an addition to their inventory worth a few thousand dollars at a cost of around $200.

At bigger sales, the FOL may host a "preview" sale for members only. It's usually well worth the $20 or so in annual dues to get in on the preview sale. Finding one gem will pay for your annual dues, and you'll also have the chance to schmooze with your fellow booksellers and collectors. Get your name on the mailing list of all the FOL groups in your region so you'll know about upcoming sales.

Many libraries also have a small daily book sale at a shelf or cart near the lobby, and some larger library systems even operate a full-time used bookstore. Sometimes these stores, tucked away in a library basement, are unadvertised gold mines.

Some book sales are better than others, however. Where there are large populations, there are lots of books, and sales near bigger cities tend to have more potential inventory. Books are also plentiful in college towns, and lots of them get donated to college-town libraries. Transient populations near universities and military bases leave lots of their books behind when they move on too.

If you can't find good library sales in your area, try looking a bit farther afield — it may be worth the drive. Look in the newspaper classifieds and consult the Web site www.BookSaleFinder.com. Here, book sale dates are listed by city several months in advance and you can subscribe to e-mail alerts of upcoming sales. The site also has classified ads from used book buyers and sellers. If you travel out of town for a book sale, combine the trip with visits to the area's used bookshops and thrift stores. You might find an overlooked bargain.

In addition to libraries, schools and civic groups organize book sales, and these sales can include some high-quality donated stock. One caveat about book sales in general, however: the biggest and most widely advertised sales aren't necessarily the best places to find good books. Sometimes the biggest sales feature a lot of junk left over from the last sale. By contrast, sales at tiny branch libraries can be chockfull of great finds but aren't publicized except for a flyer on the lobby bulletin board.

Estate sales. Estate sales can be a big source of stock but are more hit-and-miss than library sales. Normally advertised in newspaper ads, these sales liquidate the entire contents of a household and can include large book collections.

If you attend an estate sale, plan on being the first in the door. This can mean standing in line for 45 minutes or more at a well-publicized sale, but getting first crack at the books can be worth the wait.

Most estate sales are held on Friday or Saturday mornings. Larger sales may begin on Thursday and continue through Sunday. Remaining items are usually marked down 50 percent on the last day, so a good sale may be worth a second visit. But don't pass up good finds on Friday or Saturday because you think you'll get them cheaper on Sunday. By then, 98 percent of the cream will be skimmed. Get the good stuff while you can.

If there are more estate sales advertised on a given Saturday than you have time to attend, it's worth doing some detective work to determine which sales are likely to have the best books. The newspaper ad should have a contact number for the liquidator running the sale. Phone ahead and ask what types of books are available and how many. Don't rely on the newspaper ad, which might prominently mention "books" among the sale items, when only a dozen cheap paperbacks are available. Likewise, sometimes the ad won't mention books at all, but the estate owner's basement is stacked to the ceiling with collectible volumes.

Books at estate sales are about twice as expensive as those at library sales, and at $3 to $5 a pop, you'll need to be more selective because your mistakes will be costlier. If good books are on sale, try negotiating a volume discount. Instead of $3 per book, for example, ask to pay $25 for 15 books.

If estate sales work well for you, it's worthwhile to cultivate a relationship with the estate liquidators who work the sales in your area. Leave your business card and ask to be notified of all sales involving books. These contacts may also be able to alert you to book collections that come up for sale outside the estate liquidation process.

Thrift shops. Thrift shops can be worthwhile for book scouting if the store gets new stock in often enough. Unfortunately, some charity thrifts like Goodwill stores have begun selling their best donated books online. If the stock has been cherry-picked already, it's not going to be worth the time.

Church thrift shops are a potential source of stock too, however. The prices are usually reasonable and the donated books are often of higher quality than those at commercial thrift shops.

Used bookstores. A brick-and-mortar shop can be a profit center for experienced online sellers. Many walk-in stores don't have all their inventory online, and you can find pricing discrepancies. Certain books sell for significantly higher prices online than in a local used bookshop. To take but one example, a sharp book scout can regularly find copies of Nickerson's *How I Turned $1,000 into Five Million in Real Estate* in used book-shops for $10 to $15. The online price is $140.

Remainder distributors. Publisher overstocks and bookstore returns can be a profitable source of inventory for online booksellers. Unlike library sales, however, where you might routinely find good books while blind-folded, you'll need to be very cautious when buying re-mainders.

The advantage of adding remainders as a sideline to your used-book trade is the potential for expanding volume and profits. However, the average profit margin will be lower than for used books, and you must research the available titles beforehand to avoid buying titles that are too common online and priced low.

Each year, about 20,000 titles go out of print and about 25 million books are remaindered. When sales begin to slack off for a given title, big bookstore chains return much of their inventory to publishers for credit. Since publishers aren't in the business of selling individual books, they unload the remainders for pennies on the dollar. But just because remaindered books didn't sell fast enough for the chains doesn't mean you can't make money with them. You'll need to research which of the available titles remain reasonably steady sellers and are still worth half their cover price online. More on that later.

Postal Service auctions. The U.S. Postal Service (USPS) conducts public auctions at mail recovery centers around the country to liquidate unclaimed, damaged, and claim-paid merchandise. On approximately half of the sale dates, about 12 annually, the auctions consist only of bulk book lots. The lots are anywhere from 400 to 800 books and weigh several hundred pounds. Most of the books are like-new or brand-new items that have simply come unpackaged and separated from the delivery address in the mail. Bulk book lots are potluck, however — there's no list of the titles contained therein. Sometimes the lots include miscellaneous books, and sometimes they'll be only textbooks, children's books, or cookbooks, for example. The value of the individual books can range from practically nothing to hundreds of dollars. These auctions can present good buys, but whether it is worth your while will depend on what is included in the lot and how high the bidding goes.

Within the past year or so, the Postal Service has been conducting its book auctions only at its Atlanta Mail Recovery Center, and to further complicate things, some of the lots sold there must be picked up in Saint Paul, Minnesota. However, the trip can be worth your time and expense.

In addition to auctions, the Postal Service occasionally conducts sales of personal property or its own equipment. These sales are conducted at regular post offices and advertised in local newspapers. Local police departments conduct similar sales of recovered stolen merchandise that has gone unclaimed. Check the classifieds to determine if any to be held in your area include books.

To be placed on mailing lists to receive notices of postal auctions and sales, write a letter expressing interest to these offices:

San Francisco MSC
395 Oyster Point Blvd., Suite 205
So. San Francisco, CA 94099-6260

Chicago MSC
150 South Wacker Dr., Suite 200
Chicago, IL 60606-4100

Memphis MSC
225 North Humphreys Blvd.
Memphis, TN 38166-6260

Windsor MSC
8 Griffin Rd. North
Windsor, CT 06095-1572
Atlanta Mail Recovery Center
5345 Fulton Industrial Blvd., SW
Atlanta, GA 30378-2400

St Paul Mail Recovery Center
443 Fillmore Ave.
St Paul, MN 55107-9607

More information is available on the Postal Service's Web site: www.usps.com/auctions.

Treasury Department auctions. The U.S. Customs Service regularly auctions off property it has seized for trade violations, trademark or copyright violations, smuggling, drug trafficking, money laundering, and other crimes. The auctioned property includes all sorts of items and sometimes includes large lots of books, CDs, or movies. Such lots are usually listed under the "general merchandise" category.

Most Customs auctions are conducted in New Jersey, Texas, California, and Arizona. It is possible to get a good buy on merchandise at these sales, but as is the case with any auction, the final price for items depends on public interest and what people are willing to pay for them. It's a good idea to go early and inspect the merchandise. Payment is due at the auction. For more information, see the Treasury Department's Web site: www.treas.gov/auctions/customs.

Book fairs. Fairs featuring rare and antiquarian books are less frequent than they used to be because much of the trade has migrated online. Attendance has dropped off at smaller and regional book fairs within the past decade.

An increasingly common type of book fair is the "bargain book" fair. This might be a temporary sale conducted in a vacant store or mall parking lot, and the stock includes publisher overstocks and bookstore returns. The "bargain" price doesn't mean these books can be sold profitably online, however. Books being unloaded in this fashion are usually in oversupply online, and prices are therefore low. If you're tempted to buy volumes at such outlets, check the online price first.

Bargain tables. The superstore chains such as Barnes & Noble and Borders continuously offer a selection of bargain or "remainder" books discounted 50 percent to 75 percent off retail at the front of the store. It's possible to find some gems here that can be resold online.

Sometimes you'll see first editions on the remainder table, and even copies signed by the author. Depending on the author, you may be able to sell these a few years later as collectibles.

Classified ads. If you have trouble finding enough stock using the sources discussed above, try a classified advertisement.

If you place an ad offering to pay people cash, you'd better be ready for a response. The challenge is keeping the nuisance responses to a minimum. Don't give anyone the impression that you're itching to spend a wad of cash on any old books. Keep expectations low. One strategy that seems to work is offering a "finder's fee" for referrals to a collection you agree to buy.

Ads in metropolitan daily newspapers are costly, so look for alternatives such as weekly newspapers and circulars like *Penny Saver* and *Thrifty Nickel*. Another option is Craig's List at www.craigslist.com. The home page displays ads for the San Francisco Bay area, but there may be a link to your region on the right side of the page. The site has become extremely popular within the past few years, and Craig's List pages for most metro areas include several listings for bulk book buyers and sellers.

Lower priority sources

The sources listed below are those that tend to yield the fewest salable books per hour you spend searching. To stay as profitable as possible, you need to focus on the sources that work the best, where you consistently find books. The places below should be your last priority.

Garage sales and **yard sales**. Weekend neighborhood sales can be an acceptable source of stock if you enjoy wheeling and dealing. Garage and yard sales require lots of legwork though, and the proportion of junk to gems is high.

The main problem is that these sales are full of the stuff people no longer want, which contrasts with an estate sale that liquidates the entire contents of a household. Some yard salers have caught on to this difference and now advertise their garage sales as "estate sales," aiming to draw more buyers. When you're scanning the classifieds, beware of yard sales masquerading as estate sales. An "estate sale" that does not advertise items like antique furniture, silver, and stemware might be a yard sale in disguise.

Bulk lots. Each and every day there are hundreds of bulk lots of used books up for auction on eBay. The lots are usually described as someone's personal collection, but it is more likely that the books are the deadwood from some other online bookseller's inventory. These bulk lots can be a great deal for book readers but usually not for booksellers. Anyone going to the trouble to list the lot on eBay will also go to the trouble of cherry-picking the lot and keeping the best of it.

One way you might be able to get a deal on an eBay used book lot is limiting your search to sellers in your area, where you can inspect the lot before bidding.

Books on consignment. If enough people know you're a bookseller, eventually someone may ask you to sell some of their books. Presumably, you'd earn a commission on sales, and this option can be a tempting way to acquire inventory, but it carries pitfalls and can be a distraction. To do it right, you'd need to set up a bookkeeping system for consignments. You would also need good insurance coverage if you had stock on hand that you didn't own in the event of fire, flood, or some other disaster.

If books offered for consignment look good to you, offer to buy them outright. Sell them yourself and avoid the hassles of a consignment deal, which is seldom a great idea for any business. Television shows such as *Antiques Roadshow* have convinced too many people that treasures are lurking in their attic or basement. Most of the stuff isn't valuable, it's just old. You don't want to be roped into storing someone's worthless books.

What Books to Buy

To make your business highly profitable, you must hone your skill in finding unusual titles — books that are scarce enough to sell for $25, $50, and more. Finding just a few of these gems each month will have a big impact on your bottom line.

Along the way, you'll stay busy picking up general interest books for a dollar or two and reselling them for seven or eight dollars — but avoid the common books. A bestseller generally can't be resold online profitably unless the book is still fairly new. Once demand slacks off, prices will fall below $2 very quickly.

By contrast, out-of-print books can be worth several times their original cover price. I'm not necessarily talking about rare or antiquarian books here — that's a category for later discussion. Here I'm talking about books like *Cards as Weapons*, a 1977 paperback by Ricky Jay. It teaches card-scaling, the art of throwing playing cards, a skill that is apparently always in demand by amateur magicians, card sharks, and hobbyists. The book sells for $250 online, but it's likely to be priced at 50 cents at a library sale. This is exactly the kind of quirky book you should look for.

Learn to find unusual books

Below is a partial list of the titles I have purchased for a few dollars and sold online for more than $100, sometimes *substantially* more. Examine the list and consider each title and how different it is from 99.9 percent of the books you come across. The objective here is not to memorize all the titles so that you can look for them this weekend, but to begin developing your sixth sense for recognizing esoteric books.

- *The Social Psychology of Telecommunications,* by Short
- *Curves and Their Properties,* by Yates
- *Hydrocarbon Habitat in Rift Basins,* by Lambiase
- *Introduction to Management Science Deterministic Models,* by Teichroew
- *Principles of Aperture and Array System Design: Including Random and Adaptive,* by Steinberg
- *Synthetic Aperture Radar Systems: Theory and Design,* by Harger
- *Symmetrical Components, As Applied to the Analysis of Unbalanced Electrical,* by Wagner
- *The Theory of Public Finance: A Study in Public Economy ,* by Musgrave
- *Statistics for Economics: An Intuitive Approach ,* by Caniglia
- *Theory of Elastic Stability,* by Timoshenko
- *Outrageous Misconduct: The Asbestos Industry on Trial,* by Brodeur

- *Studies in the New Experimental Aesthetics: Steps Toward an Objective Psychology of Aesthetic Appreciation,* by Berlyne

- *Cross-Examination: Science & Techniques,* by Pozner

- *The Conceptual Development of Quantum Mechanics,* by Jammer

- *Collecting and Classifying Coloured Diamonds,* by Hofer

- *Interregional and International Trade,* by Ohlin

The trouble with fiction. Unless you already have expertise in fiction collecting, nonfiction is the safest area in which to begin building your inventory of used books.

The big publishers don't overprint nonfiction titles to the same degree they do fiction, so values hold steadier. Also, nonfiction tends to hold more value in the used market because readers *need* nonfiction books. These are the books that explain how to get a job, fix your car, or use the computer. Successful nonfiction books save the reader time and money.

Fiction books, by contrast, compete for the reader's leisure time. For example, there are more than 3,700 used paperback copies of John Grisham's *The Firm* for sale on Amazon Marketplace these days, with hundreds priced at one cent. Unless your copy is signed by Grisham, it's best to donate it to your local public library.

Make scarce, out-of-print books the mainstay of your business. Today's blockbuster fiction novel will probably be in demand for 6 months to a year, but a quality nonfiction title will sell steadily year after year.

Textbooks. Used textbooks are overlooked by many online sellers, who complain that their value plunges as soon as a new edition is printed. True, prices drop when a new edition appears, but that doesn't necessarily mean you can't profit by selling used textbooks. And vintage texts, particularly graduate-level mathematics and economics books, can be scarce and valuable. University professors, authors, and researchers buy many out-of-print books online — so don't rule out textbooks. Like any other nonfiction category, a certain number are scarce and valuable.

Textbooks to avoid. Introductory sociology and political science texts quickly become oversupplied online when students begin unloading last semester's books. These are the courses that nearly every freshman takes, so the textbooks are printed in huge quantities, and there's no market for such books after a new edition is printed. Because it's introductory material, this information is in several other books that are also readily available.

Study guides, introductory economics, and computer books are rarely worth much after a couple of years. By contrast, biology texts are revised less frequently than any other text category, so their value holds much steadier.

Nonfiction to avoid. Some nonfiction books have particularly low appeal in the used marketplace and are best avoided: Time-Life series, Readers Digest condensed books, and most National Geographic titles. Sports, popular art, and coffee-table tourist books are usually deadwood for the online seller. When new, these books are strong sellers, but hardly anyone wants a used one.

Business and investing books are fertile ground for online sellers, as long as the material isn't too dated and the book was not a mega-seller. Sometimes events can make these books losers overnight. For example, after the stock market crash in 2000, it became almost impossible to sell books about day-trading, a category that had been white-hot the previous few years.

Self-improvement is a strong category, as long as it's not a fad book by a celebrity. Biographies are marginal material most of the time, and memoirs of political figures, especially dead ones, are best left alone.

The history category produces several blockbusters every year, but used copies sell slowly a couple of years after release. Certain historical topics are always strong performers, however: The Civil War, World War II, Vietnam, and anything on the Confederacy. Don't bother with World War I.

Like fiction, certain nonfiction categories must be very current to sell. Don't buy travel books unless it's this year's edition. The same goes for law books.

An area where many sellers can carve out a specialty is in cookbooks. Titles in specialized categories such as bread baking, diet cooking, natural foods, and ethnic cooking are ripe for exploration. A good reference is *Cookbooks Worth Collecting,* by Mary Barile. Used microwave cookbooks are to be avoided, however — you can't even give them away.

Other books to avoid

Romance novels. Romance novels will sell quickly if they are brand new, but if you're going to sell romance novels for profit, you'll need to be a romance reader yourself. That's the only way you'll know which ones are worth carrying in your inventory.

Books by comedians. Books by comedians like Bill Cosby, Paul Reiser and Jeff Foxworthy are usually big sellers when new and make great gifts. But the books are generally overprinted and don't have much resale value a short time after printing.

Paperbacks. Mass market paperbacks are tempting to the beginning online seller because of their low purchase cost, and because they are lightweight and can be shipped cheaply. Unfortunately, the online price is quite low for most pocket books more than a few years old. You can better spend your time searching for out-of-print books worth real money.

When a title is selling for under a dollar online, that means not only that the title is oversupplied but that demand is low. Do not hang onto this type of junk hoping to make a bit of profit from shipping and handling. Over time, as your inventory expands and storage space shrinks, those cheap paperbacks taking shelf space will be a serious burden. Deleting deadwood from your online store and discarding it from your storage space is a tedious, time-consuming affair. This is a chore you can avoid by investing in quality stock now.

The larger-format "trade paperbacks" are a bit less common and can be profitable, but cheap books will come back to haunt you for other reasons as well. It just so happens that the customers who buy the cheapest books are usually your most demanding buyers. The customer who paid less than a dollar for a book is the customer who complains the loudest about shipping fees and delivery times.

Another special category is vintage paperbacks, which are quite collectible. Certain authors, cover artists, series, or genres have legions of fans. Avon, Gold Medal, and Dell "mapbacks" are in demand, so don't automatically trash old paperbacks without a glance at the cover. Every day, thousands of collectible paperbacks are thrown out or mistakenly sold for a small fraction of their collectible value, which can reach $500. A good resource is *Collectable Paperback Books,* by Canja.

Know what buyers want. Sometimes a book is in such hot demand and the supply is so low that a "buyers waiting" list is formed on Amazon Marketplace. Every day, 2,000 to 3,000 buyers "pre-order" an item, hoping that a seller will come along with an available copy. Buyers indicate the title, price, and condition of the item they want to purchase. In some cases, these buyers want a book at an unreasonably low price. But in most cases, the buyers-waiting list indicates those titles where demand has outstripped supply. If you have an Amazon account, you can download a buyers-waiting report at this address: https://secure.amazon.com/exec/panama/seller-admin/download/preorder-report/002-7098957-4009620.

Sellers who list lots of inventory will regularly stumble onto these buyers-waiting situations. If you list an item for sale through the "Sell Yours Here" button, and there is at least one buyer with a pre-order, when you reach the page to indicate your price you'll see an orange box on the right labeled "BUYER WAITING." There might also be a message indicating, for example, "Average pending pre-order price (based on your condition) $20." You should price your item at least double the average pre-order price. If it remains unsold after a week or so at that price, you can always lower it incrementally to find the exact price that will trigger one of the pre-orders.

How much to pay. How much should you pay for your stock? You should have no trouble limiting your costs to $2 or $3 per book by buying at library sales. It's hard to get into serious trouble when you're spending only a few dollars per book. If you're fairly resourceful in finding books and decent at picking them, you should pay about $1.75 per book on average, and your average sale should be about $11.

A good rule of thumb is to try to triple your money when acquiring stock. Remember that commissions, shipping costs, and items that don't sell will cut into that margin. But like every rule, this one has exceptions. If you find a book you know you'll be able to sell quickly at $100, do not hesitate to pay $60 to get it. It's a lot easier to make $40 on one sale than it is to make $5 on each of eight separate transactions.

Nobody bets right all the time, and no matter how good you are at picking books, if you're just working on hunches you will inevitably accumulate some losers and pass up winners. However, if you have a Web-enabled cell phone, it's now possible to research book prices even while you're at a sale. You can even hook up a scanner to some of these phones so you don't need to type in the ISBNs. This type of tool can take some of the pure joy out of finding great books through serendipity, but it can also help your bottom line. See the section on Advanced Automation for a list of vendors of wireless price-lookup services.

Where to Sell Books

Auction marketplaces like eBay captured most of the early online bookselling volume during the 1990s. But much of the business has migrated to fixed-price platforms, and today, the real action is on Amazon Marketplace.

Auctions can be fun for high-priced items, but when it comes down to it, most book buyers would rather just buy the book and be done with it. Although some booksellers still prefer auctions for truly rare books, hoping that a bidding war will erupt, a growing number of sellers are opting to park all their inventory on fixed-price marketplaces like Amazon, and wait for the right buyer to come along.

A well-greased marketplace like Amazon works as a *reverse* auction. Instead of buyers competing to offer the highest price, sellers compete to offer the lowest price.

Amazon Marketplace. Amazon is the 800-pound gorilla of online bookselling, with tens of millions of preregistered buyers. In May 2005, the site had 41 million visitors, compared with 35.5 million a year earlier. Amazon sellers have no-cost access to the world's biggest online book bazaar, paying a commission to Amazon only after a sale.

The biggest advantage for Amazon sellers is that used merchandise is displayed right alongside Amazon's new items. So buyers looking for new books discover the used and collectible items at the same time. In just a few years, this has added millions of buyers to used-book trading.

If you are just getting into online bookselling, it is best to work exclusively on Amazon while you learn the business. Most books will sell faster and at higher prices on Amazon than anywhere else on the Internet. Later, you can decide if it's worthwhile to increase sales a bit by listing your inventory on more venues, but first, you'll need a system for keeping your inventory current to prevent multiple customers from buying the same book on different sites.

Amazon is also the most user-friendly site for beginners. You can simply use the "Sell Yours Here" button displayed on any product page, or for a step-by-step tutorial on listing items for sale at Marketplace, see the quick start guide, www.amazon.com/exec/obidos/tg/browse/-/1161234.

After you open your seller account, Amazon will deposit funds from your sales into the bank account you designate. You'll also receive a shipping credit that will cover your shipping costs in most cases.

Fees. In addition to its 15-percent commission, Amazon tacks on another $1.23 per transaction, which is apparently used to cover refunds issued through its A-to-Z buyers' guarantee program. Also, a 99-cent fee applies to all sales except those made by Pro-Merchant Subscribers.

Amazon Pro-Merchant Subscription. For a fee of $39.99 a month, Amazon provides access to bulk selling tools and waives the 99-cent fee charged on Marketplace sales. For sellers with more than 40 sales per month, the subscription pays for itself.

Amazon zShops. The precursor to Marketplace was zShops, which was launched in 1999 to provide small businesses with storefronts on Amazon. The idea was to make Amazon a venue where practically any type of merchandise in the world could be traded, but most Amazon buyers find items through searches and do not browse through shops or categories. The shops are not highly customizable, nor are they promoted by Amazon, so their utility is limited. The shops can be used to sell items that Amazon hasn't authorized for sale on Marketplace, however. The zShops program is open only to Pro-Merchant subscribers. For items under $25, sellers pay a 5 percent closing fee.

Amazon auctions. When it launched its auction platform in 1999, Amazon hoped to lure auction fans from eBay. At the time, experts predicted that auctions might become the dominant form of online commerce.

After a lukewarm response from buyers, however, Amazon quit publicizing its auctions. Today, Amazon's auction platform is practically invisible to buyers and most sellers have abandoned auctions.

Half.com, at www.Half.com, appeared to be poised to rival Amazon and eBay as an online trading hub for books and music just a few years ago. It combined the best features of the bigger rivals — a community of buyers and sellers like eBay's with simple Amazon-like fixed-priced trading.

Then eBay bought Half.com and was expected to make a run at Amazon's fixed-price trading dominance. Instead, Amazon simply copied all the best features of Half and called it Amazon Marketplace. After Amazon siphoned off most of Half's traffic, eBay announced plans to close Half in 2004. Sellers were encouraged to move their listings to eBay stores, which offered lower fees and fixed-price trading. After an outcry from sellers, however, eBay relented and Half remains open. But the site hasn't been promoted for some time, and sales are down to a trickle.

Fees. Half charges sellers a 15-percent commission, slightly less for items priced over $50.

Biblio, at www.biblio.com, is one of the most recently launched used bookselling sites, but it already claims to be among the top three. It hosts about 3,000 member book dealers from 24 countries offering 25 million books. The company boosted its volume in 2003 by buying out a competitor, Bookopoly.

Biblio charges members a sliding commission based on how many listings are active and the value of sales. In general, the sellers pay 15 percent on their first few hundred dollars in monthly sales, then 7.5 percent on monthly sales over that amount. In addition, credit card processing costs 5 percent of the overall transaction plus an additional 25 cents.

eBay, at www.ebay.com, was popular for book dealers when the Internet first went mainstream in the mid-1990s. But growth is slowing, and many booksellers have quit using the auction format for common books.

Bookseller gripes against eBay have mounted for some time. It seems that bidding volume goes down and fees go up each year. The listing process is more complicated than ever. "Not enough buyers and too many sellers" is a common refrain on eBay these days.

The biggest drawback with eBay when compared to Amazon is that eBay requires so much more time for the same level of sales and yet generates more aggravation in the form of problem customers. Non-paying buyers and quibbling about shipping rates are a particular problem. One remedy for this is to demand immediate payment via PayPal for all transactions, but this precaution generates still more e-mails from buyers demanding to mail a check.

Booksellers have had mixed success selling their wares in eBay stores. A major early beef was that store items weren't visible in buyers' search results. In a bid to save its Stores program, it seems that eBay is beginning to listen to the complaints from booksellers. Store items have been added to search results, and eBay has begun exporting store inventories to other platforms like Froogle, Yahoo, and Shopping.com.

Fees. eBay has a complicated schedule of fees. Generally, for an item selling at around $25, you'll pay an insertion fee of 60 cents plus a final-value fee of 5.25 percent. More fees are due for Buy-It-Now, pictures, and other bells and whistles. If you use PayPal, there are more fees. See the menu of eBay fees at this address: http://pages.ebay.com/help/sell/fees.html.

Abebooks.com, at www.abebooks.com. The Advanced Book Exchange was the first big online database for online booksellers, arriving on the scene in the 1990s. Its major competitor was Bibliofind, which was later bought by Amazon. Abebooks says it has about 13,000 members with 70 million listings and 1.5 million registered buyers. Just five years ago, more than 90 percent of online booksellers were Abebooks members, but with the advent of Amazon Marketplace, Abebooks now appears to control less than 25 percent of today's seller corps.

Abebooks sellers pay a basic subscription fee of $25 monthly, but the fee rises based on the number of listings. Sellers with more than 500 listings pay $37 a month and the fee can go up to $300 for those with more than 15,000 listings. A commission of 8 percent of the book's price is paid on each sale, up to a maximum of $40 per book. The minimum commission is 50 cents per book. If Abebooks processes a credit card transaction, there is a fee of 5.5 percent.

The disadvantage of Abebooks for buyers is that it produces an uneven shopping experience compared with standardized marketplaces like Amazon and Half. Sellers may also have their own shipping and return policies.

Alibris, at www.alibris.com, evolved from BookQuest, an early business-to-business network for antiquarian book dealers. It charges sellers a 15-percent commission on the sale of items priced under $500 and 10 percent on items over $500. Sellers are also charged a minimum monthly subscription fee of $15, and the fee can rise to $150 a month for sellers with more than 100,000 listings. Alternatively, sellers can pay $1 per item sold instead of the monthly subscription fee. The company also sells and warehouses some used books on its own. One advantage of Alibris is that it allows sellers to target business and library customers.

Barnes & Noble, at www.bn.com, is the second-largest online bookseller, though it trails Amazon by a huge margin. B&N has been experimenting with adding a third-party sellers' platform like Amazon's Marketplace. For a while during 2004, ABE members could list used books for sale on its Web site, but the listings are pretty well hidden and B&N has a moratorium on new sellers. The situation bears watching, however. B&N is the leading brick-and-mortar book chain and could shake things up if it launches a real used-book marketplace.

A1Books, at www.a1books.com, launched an online bookselling marketplace in 2004. The company is part of A1Overstock, a distributor of remainder books. The Web site is well designed, and several big sellers are participating, but it's unclear whether the buyers have arrived.

A1 Marketplace has about 2,000 sellers, who pay a commission of 12 percent on sales. Proceeds from sales are transmitted to sellers via PayPal.

TomFolio.com, at www.tomfolio.com, was launched in 1999 as a platform for trading used, rare, and collectible books, as well as ephemera and periodicals. This company is organized as a cooperative and was designed as a refuge for independent sellers who wanted to operate free of corporate influence. The site appeals especially to specialist dealers.

TomFolio charges a monthly listing fee of $35 for up to 4,000 listings, and the fee rises to $90 for sellers with more than 75,000 listings.

BookAvenue.com, at www.bookavenue.com, is a site for dealers of out-of-print, used, and rare books. The subscription fee ranges from $5 per month for up to 200 listings to $49.95 for more than 100,000 listings. The subscription fee is waived for the first three months.

UsedBookCentral, www.usedbookcentral.com, charges a monthly fee based on the number of listings — $17.50 for up to 25,000 listings and $37.50 for more than 50,000. Sellers pay no commissions. Members receive a free home page with logos and custom text.

Halfvalue.com, at www.halfvalue.com, is a relative newcomer that got some buzz when eBay announced plans to close its Half.com site in 2004. Halfvalue imitates several themes from its larger rivals, including the "Half" name and Amazon's "Sell Yours Here" button and "A-to-Z" buyer guarantee.

Halfvalue sellers pay a 15-percent commission and 79-cent transaction fee on each sale. Funds are paid twice a month via PayPal. To avoid paying the 79-cent transaction fees, volume sellers can choose to pay a $15 monthly subscription fee and may upload their inventory files electronically.

Halfvalue seems to have attracted some sellers to the site, but it remains to be seen if a critical mass of buyers is there.

Yahoo Stores at www.shopping.yahoo.com. The pioneering Web portal has made steady progress with its shopping platform and claims to host one of every eight new online stores. Three packages are offered, with the entry-level "basic" store carrying a $39.95 monthly fee, a 1.5-percent transaction fee, and a $50 setup fee. Results have been mixed according to participating booksellers.

ValoreBooks.com, at www.Valorebooks.com, targets the college textbook market. Listings are free and sales incur a 15-percent commission.

Your own Web site

Several vendors have prepackaged solutions that enable booksellers to quickly open a store on their own Web site. By keeping customers at their own Web sites, sellers can potentially avoid commissions and lose fewer sales to competitors offering the same book for a few cents less.

To build their own store, a seller must first choose from two basic designs: a PC-administered system or a Web-based administration. A Web-based store is usually easier to set up but has less flexibility. By contrast, a PC-based store has a steeper learning curve but offers greater flexibility to customize the site.

The danger is that, if your vendor fails or goes out of business, your business can go down the tubes with it.

If you have a Web-based store, your site will go down when your vendor's site is down, and if the vendor goes out of business, your store might be lost for good. A PC-based store, however, could be switched to a different Internet host if necessary. Security is also better for PC sites, since your customer data is stored offline.

The key to getting sales on your Web store is driving traffic there — buyers won't find your site unless you market it. Traffic from search engines such as Google is typically a major source of Web shoppers. A store administered on your PC may show up better in search engine results if you can customize HTML meta-tags for each product page. Web-based stores don't rank as high as PC-based stores in search engine results, so your marketing may have to rely on e-mail.

The good news is that e-mail promotion is an effective, economical marketing engine for small sellers. You can rent e-mail lists of qualified book buyers from list brokers, but the best source of e-mail addresses is your previous buyers. A comprehensive resource on the topic is *Internet Direct Mail,* by Robert W. Bly.

Be sure to provide a way for recipients to opt out of receiving your e-mails, however. You don't want to be accused of sending spam. If you market your Web site with unsolicited e-mails, you're required to comply with the CAN-SPAM Act. The law requires advertising e-mails sent to someone you don't have an existing business relationship with to:

• be identified as an advertisement

- have a valid return e-mail address
- have a legitimate subject heading
- include an opt-out or unsubscribe provision, and
- include your physical mailing address.

White Oak Books, at www.whiteoakbooks.com, is perhaps the easiest Web bookstore solution. The company will maintain your Amazon Marketplace inventory on your Web site for a modest quarterly fee. Customers leave your site only after they click the "buy from Amazon" button. Users have a control panel to adjust the look and feel of their site, and customers pay via Amazon's payment system or PayPal.

White Oak Books automatically downloads your inventory from Amazon, so your store is limited to items that are eligible for Marketplace selling.

Fees. Users pay a setup fee of $50 to $100 depending on the size of inventory, and a quarterly fee of $20 to $60. If your buyer checks out at Amazon, the customary 15-percent commission on Marketplace sales applies.

Chrislands, at www.chrislands.com, can build a Web site that enables booksellers to accept any type of payment without being assessed the usual 15-percent commission on Amazon Marketplace sales. Users can sell any books or other type of merchandise, and inventory is automatically uploaded to Froogle, the online shopping venue operated by Google.

Users upload their inventory in a file formatted in UIEE (Universal Information Exchange Environment) or with a tab- or comma-delimited text file.

Fees. Users pay a setup fee of $199.99, and a monthly fee ranging from $9.99 to $29.99 depending on the size of the inventory.

Grading and Pricing Books

Condition. The key to the salability of used and collectible books is their condition. For a rare book, the dust jacket can account for as much as 90 percent of its value as a collectible. So in most cases it's best to pass up books that have major flaws like broken bindings and missing dust jackets.

Buyers understand that a used book will show some wear, but nobody wants to receive a book that looks abused. No matter how many precautions you take to warn a customer about a book's defects, you run the risk of ending up with an unhappy buyer who didn't read the description or forgot the details. Many buyers on Amazon Marketplace, for example, do not notice the "seller's comments" area of a book's listing, the only place available to add details about your book's condition.

Sometimes condition problems will escape your attention and the customer will receive a book with blank or missing pages, for example. Don't be shocked if the customer accuses you of fraud. Lots of Marketplace buyers assume that you've just finished reading the very copy of the book you sold them. And so, the reasoning goes, if you failed to mention the condition problem, you're obviously untrustworthy.

If this happens, or I should say, *when* this happens, calmly explain that you weren't aware of the flaw. Offer a full refund and a prepaid return mailing container. It's part of the cost of doing business when you sell used books.

Each time you list new books for sale is a good opportunity to take a moment to examine them and spruce up their appearance. Thumb through the book carefully to look for highlighting or underlining. Light pencil marks can usually be completely erased with a quality eraser. Straighten any bent pages and remove any foreign objects, like bookmarks and paper clips. Remove price tags from the cover. Sticker residue and most ink stains can be removed with a solvent like Goo-Gone.

Assigning condition. As the popular marketplaces have brought used books to the masses over the past few years, the terminology used by booksellers to describe the condition of used books has simplified. The streamlined system in use today on the popular online marketplaces follows these guidelines:

- **New:** A brand new, unread copy in perfect condition. Dust cover is intact; pages are pristine; book is suitable for a gift.

- **Like New:** An apparently unused copy in perfect condition. Suitable for a gift.

- **Very Good:** A copy that has been read but is still in excellent condition. Pages are intact and contain no underlining, highlighting, or notes.

- **Good:** A good reading copy, clean, with all pages intact and dust jacket present (if issued). Spine may show some wear, and pages may include limited notes and highlighting.

- **Acceptable:** A usable copy. All pages are intact, but the dust jacket may be missing. Pages may include considerable notes or highlighting, but text must not be obscured.

Be conservative when assigning condition — your customers will appreciate it. Nothing makes a buyer happier than receiving a book in better condition than expected. Other things being equal, used books advertised as "very good" seem to sell just as fast as those rated "like new." Maybe buyers figure that sellers who aren't promising perfection are probably more honest.

The simplified bookseller terminology made popular on Amazon will suffice in most cases, but dealers of antiquarian and rare books tend to use the condition terminology made popular by sellers in the 1940s:

- **As new:** This term is to be used only when the book is in the same perfect condition as published. It is to have no defects, missing pages, or library stamps, and the dust jacket (if issued) must be in mint condition.

- **Fine:** This approaches the "as new" category, but the book is not as crisp. "Fine" must also indicate no defects, and if the jacket has a small tear or other defect or looks worn, this should be noted.

- **Very good:** This can describe a used book that shows minor wear but has no tears to the binding or paper. Any defects must be noted.

- **Good:** This describes the average used, worn book that has all pages present and no defect that obscures the text. Defects must be noted.

- **Fair:** This is a worn book with complete text pages (including those with maps or plates) but that perhaps lacks endpapers, half-title, etc. Binding and jacket may be worn. Defects must be noted.

- **Poor:** This is a book that may have considerable wear but will suffice as a reading copy because it has the complete text unobscured. It may be soiled, scuffed, or stained, or have loose joints or pages. Any defects must be noted.

- **Ex-library:** Former library books taken out of circulation must be designated as library copies, no matter what their condition.

- **Book club:** These editions must always be noted as such, no matter what the book's condition.

- **Binding copy:** This describes a book in which the pages are fine but the binding is lose or detached.

If you're selling on Amazon, don't assume that your customer is going to know bookselling jargon — and never describe a book as being "in good condition for its age." The book is in good condition or it's not.

Pricing books. When you are dealing with general stock worth modest amounts – and there are several copies listed online under $15 – there is no need to spend much time mulling pricing strategies. Supply and demand rules. If you price your copy much higher than competing offers, odds are you'll wait a long time for a sale. If you think the market price is fair, match the lowest price but don't go under. The only thing lowballing accomplishes is leaving money on the table.

But what if there are no used copies listed on Amazon? In this case it's worth your time to do some research to see what the prices are outside Amazon. Search the title on AddALL, at www.addall.com, which indexes all the major book listing sites. A similar site on which to research prices is FetchBook.Info, at www.FetchBook.info. Another favorite with online booksellers but with somewhat slow performance is BookFinder.com, at www.BookFinder.com.

If your search turns up several listings for your title, you can get a good idea of its value by throwing out the top and bottom prices and averaging the rest. Price your copy at the top of the range.

Amazon Sales Rank. Some sellers like to consider a title's Amazon sales rank in making their buying decision. The rank is a measure of how often a particular book sells compared to every other book in Amazon's catalog of more than 3 million titles.

The sales rank can be as low as 1 or higher than 3 million. The lower the number, the greater the sales volume — a sales rank of 1 designates the top-selling book on

Amazon. If you list a book for sale in the lowest 2,000 sales rank, the odds are it will sell within hours, assuming it's priced competitively.

You can look up a title's Amazon sales rank by looking in the "Product details" section of the title's Web page on Amazon. The number can change frequently, since Amazon recalculates the sales rank of books in the top 10,000 once every hour. Books ranked from 10,000 to 100,000 are assigned a new rank once per day. There are also books with no sales rank on Amazon, which means that no copies have sold.

Since Amazon has an estimated 70-percent share of the Internet book market, its sales rankings are the best free information about book sales. Amazon made a series of changes in October 2004 to make its sales rank system more accurate and transparent. The rankings now take sales of new and used Marketplace items and e-books into account.

All this does not mean you should rule out books with high sales ranks, say more than 400,000. If you're the only seller with a copy, you'll get the sale. You might have to wait a year for a buyer to come along, but if you price high, it will be worth the wait.

Amazon does not publicly discuss its sales figures for individual titles, but a number of outsiders have attempted to calculate what a given sales rank means in terms of quantity sold. A book with an average sales rank of 1,000 sells about 90 copies a week, while a book with an average rank of 500,000 sells about one copy per week, according to statistics compiled by Morris Rosenthal, publisher of Foner Books. Rosenthal figures that an Amazon sales rank of 10,000 translates into two sales per day, and a sales rank of 1 million translates into a single sale every other month.

In other research, economists at MIT figured that a book ranked number 10 on Amazon sells about 5,000 copies on Amazon each week, and a book with a rank of 100,000 sells 1.6 copies per week on average. Amazon sells more than 100 million books per year, and about half of those unit sales come from sales of titles ranking above 40,000, according to the MIT research. Titles ranked from 100,000 to 200,000 account for just 7.3 percent of sales at Amazon, and titles ranked from 200,000 to 300,000 produce just 4.6 percent of sales.

Slower-selling books tend to have higher prices, according to the MIT researchers. They found that the average price of books with a sales rank higher than 100,000 is about $8 higher than the faster-selling titles.

JungleScan, at www.JungleScan.com, is a free Web site that tracks the Amazon sales rank of any book over time and can display a graph of the data similar to a stock chart. Registering for a free account allows you to create your own "portfolio" of books to track.

JungleScan's home page features the titles that experienced the biggest jump in sales for that day, which are usually those that have been mentioned in the national media. For example, if a book author appears on Oprah Winfrey's television show or is mentioned in a front-page newspaper story, the sales of the book will spike for several days.

Title Z, at www.TitleZ.com, is a more elaborate, fee-based sales charting service. It allows users to instantly retrieve historic and current sales rankings from Amazon and create printable reports with 7-day, 30-day, 90-day, and lifetime averages. The idea is to see how topics or titles perform over time compared to competing titles.

Adjusting prices. One distasteful chore for online booksellers is cutting prices to keep their listings competitive. Not all buyers choose the lowest price, but it's clear that listings must be visible in the marketplace to sell. Books priced far above the market price are effectively hidden and extremely unlikely to sell. Most buyers will not look past the first few listings displayed, simply because they do not realize there is another choice, and the rest don't want to make the effort.

This situation can bring out the stubbornness in some sellers, who refuse to sell a book for less than they paid for it. Forget what you paid for each book. You don't win every time, and the important thing is your average profit margin and cash flow.

Clearing deadwood. Each time you list a new batch of books you've purchased, you can assume that about 25 percent should sell within three months. Within about 18 months, 65 percent to 75 percent of those books will probably have sold, depending on your pricing strategy and buyer demand for the titles you picked.

Now is the time to begin determining which of the remaining stock is deadwood and must be removed from inventory. A good starting point is a price of $10. If books are priced below that point, out they go after 18 months. Deadwood sitting in your inventory costs you money. The space the book is occupying could be used by newer inventory that will bring in profits. Be brutal. Clear space on your shelf for new inventory that will generate cash.

More patience is appropriate for higher-priced books, however. Obscure books priced more than $50 may take two or three years to find a buyer.

Once storage space becomes tight and you've confronted the nuisance of clearing deadwood, the need for selective buying will be more obvious. It takes time and effort to cull the losers, time you could be spending finding profitable books. Set guidelines you feel are appropriate for your situation. For example, you might decide to reject books you can't sell for more than $6.

Keep working. When the storage space some sellers envisioned for their business becomes full, they lose momentum. They let the deadwood sit and they slack off on book buying — and then they start griping about slow sales. The reason sales are slow is that their inventory is stale.

If you're still short on space after you've cleaned out your deadwood, rent more space at a local storage facility. If you're buying the right books, the profits will cover rent on storage space many times over.

What do you do with the books you need to unload? Donate them to a charity or a thrift store. You can also try selling your discards as a bulk lot on eBay or in Amazon's zShops. eBay bulk sellers often have more luck by dividing lots into similar interest categories. For example, instead of selling a "pot luck" set of 50 unnamed books, you'll get more bids by dividing the pile into separate lots of 15 romance novels, 20 business books, and 15 cookbooks. Post a picture of the lot and name the titles.

You can also try trading in your deadwood for new books at a local used bookstore. Some titles that are over-supplied online sell steadily in a brick-and-mortar shop. Try to get store credit and trade up for higher-quality stock.

Focus on Service

Many used booksellers like to think of themselves as retailers, but a better approach is to think of your business as a *service*. You're selling convenience and service just as much as you're selling books. Most of your sales will come from new customers, and the only way to differentiate yourself from competitors is the "feedback" record you earn by providing good service to buyer after buyer.

Feedback. All the major online trading venues have a "feedback" system designed to enable transaction partners who don't know each other to predict one another's likely performance. Sellers who are able to build a positive feedback record have a huge advantage over competitors and can command higher prices than lower-ranked competitors.

Buyers who consult feedback ratings on Amazon Marketplace will concern themselves mainly with the "At a Glance" page, which summarizes the percentages for positive, negative, and neutral ratings for sellers over four time periods: 30 days, 90 days, 365 days and lifetime.

A perfect score is 100, and careful sellers can expect to keep their positive feedback averages in the mid-90s on Amazon. Half.com and eBay sellers can easily keep their positive feedback average in the high 90s, given that eBay buyers are much more reluctant to leave negative ratings. Unlike on Amazon, feedback averages on eBay and Half include ratings by sellers.

Sellers gripe about feedback systems, which are always imperfect, but feedback can serve as a useful tool for managing your business. By aiming to minimize negative feedback, you'll automatically be focused on preventing mistakes that cost money to correct.

The best way to prevent bad feedback is to have a daily routine for managing your business. For example, morning can be a good time to check your e-mails and answer inquiries received overnight. Prompt communication with buyers prevents small problems from growing into big problems.

Having satisfied customers is fine, but the real payoff comes through future rewards of repeat sales. Satisfied customers come back again and again, and that's the lifeblood of every successful business.

So to maintain your level of service and minimize negative feedback, focus on the things you can control: prompt shipping, careful communication, and accurate descriptions.

Prompt shipping. Buyers expect prompt shipment and a confirmation of shipment. Part-time sellers can probably get by shipping two or three times per week, but if you take your business seriously, commit yourself to shipping on a daily basis. Aim higher than the minimum requirements.

Justified or not, more than half of buyer feedback comments will mention the delivery time. "Prompt delivery" and "I received it in a few days" are typical feedback comments from satisfied customers. "Very slow" is a typical feedback comment, and obviously, the customer could actually be rating the Postal Service rather than the seller.

So it's unavoidable that seller ratings will suffer from slow delivery and other issues outside your control. The best way to minimize problems from delivery speed is shipping as promptly as possible. Daily shipping is not required but will result in more on-time deliveries, and so it's in your long-term interest.

On most selling venues, buyers have two U.S. Postal Service shipping options: standard (Media Mail) and expedited (Priority Mail). Customers rarely choose to pay for expedited shipping, but they frequently complain when standard shipping fails to arrive within a week or so.

So the problem is that the vast majority of used book buyers select standard shipping, but a significant portion, about 5 percent, don't consider the service adequate. Two weeks is no longer an acceptable delivery time in the eyes of many buyers, who have grown accustomed to the shorter UPS and FedEx delivery timeframes provided on most mail-order deliveries.

To minimize grief over tardy Media Mail packages, some sellers give free upgrades on all standard orders to Priority Mail. The logic is that spending about $2 extra on each package is an acceptable price for eliminating all bad feedback and e-mail inquiries related to delivery time. But let's look at the long-term financial impact of free shipping upgrades.

Suppose "Seller A" ships an average of 30 books daily, and three of those customers pay to upgrade to expedited shipping. For the remaining 27 orders, Seller A upgrades the shipping at his own expense, at a cost of $54 a day.

"Seller B" receives the same rate of orders, 30 per day, with three customers paying for Priority Mail. For the other 27 orders, Seller B provides Media Mail shipping, just what the customer paid for.

The table below shows the cumulative cost over one year of free shipping upgrades.

Seller A

Daily postage costs for 30 Priority Mail flat rate envelopes: 30 x $3.85 = $115.50

Annual postage cost: Daily cost x 5 days per week x 52 weeks per year = **$30,030**

Seller B

Daily postage costs for 27 Media Mail packages: 27 x $1.42 = $38.34

Daily postage costs for 3 Priority Mail flat rate envelopes: 3 x $3.85 = $11.55

Daily cost: $49.89

Annual postage cost: Daily cost x 5 days per week, 52 weeks per year = **$12,971**

Annual cost to Seller A for free shipping upgrades: $17,059

The free shipping upgrades cost Seller A $17,000 annually, which comes directly from his bottom line. Depending on his average net profit per sale, he might be losing as much as one-third of his net profit to the shipping policy. Viewed in that light, free shipping upgrades do not appear to be a practical solution for improving customer satisfaction.

Working with the USPS. The vast majority of sellers use the Postal Service to deliver all packages. Used book buyers tend to be price-sensitive folks, and there's not enough margin in book profits and shipping credits to pay for alternatives like UPS or FedEx.

More than 85 percent of Amazon Marketplace buyers select "standard" shipping instead of "expedited" shipping. Although we've seen that a blanket policy of free shipping upgrades isn't practical, there are special cases when it's wise for sellers to upgrade shipping automatically. Media Mail does not provide adequate service for U.S. residents outside the lower 48 states. Delivery to Alaska and Hawaii can easily take four to six weeks, which is not explained to Amazon customers when they check out with standard shipping. For these buyers, as well as overseas government and military employees with APO/FPO addresses, you would be wise to upgrade shipping to First Class or Priority Mail service whenever possible. Technically an upgrade is not required, but it's the only way to prevent tardy delivery and minimize negative feedback.

International shipping

International shipping generates more complications. Whether to offer shipping to overseas customers is a decision sellers should make according to the nature of their inventory and perhaps on a book-by-book basis.

Sellers whose stock consists primarily of inexpensive commodity-type books sometimes elect to forgo international sales in order to streamline their shipping operation. For buyers with scarce, pricey items, it's worthwhile to ship internationally to enhance cash flow and turnover.

For overseas delivery, most standard-sized books will fit into a flat-rate Postal Service Global Priority envelope. The postage cost is $8, and delivery usually takes less than a week. The cheaper alternative, "surface shipping," can take six to eight weeks for delivery to your overseas buyers. Such a lengthy wait almost always results in an angry customer. So for inexpensive books that don't fit into a Global Priority envelope, it's prudent to offer shipping only to U.S. buyers.

Send a shipment confirmation. Send your buyers an e-mail confirming the shipment on the day you ship their book. For Amazon orders, you can reach the customer by replying to the "Sold, Ship Now" e-mail that you get when an item sells.

A short message confirming the book is on the way reassures the customer and prevents unnecessary and time-consuming inquiries days later. Below is a sample script you can use to confirm shipment of an order via standard shipping. (You can store this script and others in a file on your desktop, ready for quick modification.)

Dear [Buyer Name],

Thank you for purchasing [Item]. I shipped

your package today via the U.S. Postal Service from [City]. It should arrive in about 4 to 14 business days.

You can track the delivery status here:

http://trkcnfrm1.smi.usps.com/netdata-cgi/db2www/cbd_243.d2w/output?CAMEFRO M=OK&strOrigTrackNum=[Tracking Number here]

Best regards,
Your Seller

The URL displays the delivery status on the Postal Service's Web site, which brings up my next tip:

Provide a tracking number. Because Postal Service Media Mail can take a few weeks to arrive, it's best to provide proof of shipment in the form of a delivery confirmation number. Delivery confirmation is not required but serves a number of useful purposes. It gives the buyer peace of mind and reduces the number of unnecessary e-mail inquiries you'll receive that ask about delivery status. Having proof of shipment also provides cover for sellers when the Postal Service fails to deliver the package within 30 days. If your Amazon customer files for an A-to-Z refund, providing proof of shipment to Amazon in the form of the delivery confirmation number can prevent the buyer's refund from being deducted from your account.

Delivery confirmation can also be useful for jogging the memory of buyers who received the item weeks ago but have forgotten it by the time they receive their 30-day feedback e-mail from Amazon. Sending them a friendly reminder of the day and time of the delivery tends to end the matter.

If you use an online postage service, you'll receive the discount "electronic" rate of 13 cents per delivery confirmation. That's a 37-cent savings over the "retail" rate of 50 cents you pay if you present the package to a Postal Service clerk. That is hardly an earth-shattering amount in itself, but think of the cumulative impact for a seller who ships an average of 40 parcels a day, five times per week. The annual savings would be $3,848. That's a big chunk of change to leave on the table.

Describe items accurately. Disclose any imperfections in the book and describe any markings. Be conservative when describing the condition of your inventory. For a discussion of condition guidelines, see page 48.

Enclose your contact information. A packing slip with the order number and your e-mail address will be useful in case you made a mistake filling the order or the customer receives something unexpected. For Amazon Marketplace orders, a packing slip can be printed from your order e-mails or your payments account on the Web. Third-party software tools can automate this procedure, eliminating the need for cutting and pasting. For more information, see appendix 3.

Solicit feedback <u>after</u> delivery. Encourage customers to give you a feedback rating, explaining that it will help you show other potential buyers that you're a trustworthy and reliable seller. Solicit feedback on the packing slip, not in your shipment confirmation e-mail. An early prompting in the shipping confirmation will make some customers impatient, and they might submit a negative rating before their package is due to arrive. The customer is in a better frame of mind after he receives the book.

Here's sample text you can print on your packing slip to encourage feedback after delivery:

Dear Customer:

Thank you for your purchase. If you are happy with my service, please leave "feedback" for me on Amazon.com, which will let other buyers know I'm a responsible and reliable seller. If you were unsatisfied for any reason, I would appreciate hearing from you before you leave feedback so that I might resolve any issues regarding the transaction.

You can leave feedback for me here:

https://www.amazon.com/gp/css/summary/edit.html?orderID=[order number goes here]

Best regards,

Your Seller

Notice that the message above provides another opportunity for correcting mistakes and misunderstandings before a customer submits negative feedback.

Most of the feedback sellers receive on Amazon results from the company's form e-mails, which are sent 30 days after the purchase with the subject line "Rate Your Transaction at Amazon.com." Many buyers don't bother to read the instructions, which can result in baffling or inappropriate feedback. Some buyers assume they're being asked to critique the book, the Postal Service, or Amazon's checkout process.

Some new sellers are eager to establish a track record and want feedback as soon as possible. If you would rather solicit feedback directly from your customers via e-mail before they receive the 30-day form e-mail from Amazon, here are simple instructions to send your buyer:

- *Go to http://www.amazon.com/feedback.*

- *When prompted, log into your account.*

- *You'll see a list of the orders for which you can leave feedback.*

- *Find the appropriate order on the list and click the "Leave seller feedback" button on the right.*

If you have the order ID number handy, you can give your buyer a direct link for leaving feedback:

https://www.amazon.com/gp/css/summary/edit.html?orderID=(order number goes here)

Request negative feedback removal. Protect your feedback average by asking buyers to remove negative ratings you believe are unfair. A polite request will result in feedback removal about 60 percent of the time. If the buyer cooperates and removes the rating, it will be removed from your feedback page and will no longer be counted toward your average. So it's well worth the effort.

This is where having a script on hand really helps. You're likely to be angry after receiving a negative rating, particularly from an ill-informed buyer. Your first instinct may be to give your customer an earful and try to shame them into removing feedback, but the response will likely be defensiveness and intransigence.

Below is a sample script to request removal of a negative feedback rating in cases where the buyer is unhappy about delivery time. Notice that it achieves three key objectives:

- apologizing for the slow delivery
- gently explaining that the customer received the promised service
- suggesting how the buyer can avoid the problem on future purchases.

Dear [Buyer]:

I noticed the negative feedback comment you left on my Amazon.com account regarding the delivery time of your book. I apologize that delivery took so long. However, I did ship your package within 24 hours using standard mail, as you requested on your order.

I would greatly appreciate it if you would remove the feedback comment. I'm concerned that other buyers may avoid purchasing from me after reading it.

You can remove the feedback by clicking on the "Your Account" button at the top right of www.amazon.com. Click on the "View Order" button next to our transaction. The second box down is labeled "Your feedback for [Seller Name]." There you'll see a "remove" button.

For future reference, you can ensure three-day delivery on all Marketplace purchases by selecting "expedited" shipping at checkout instead of "standard." The expedited option costs $2 extra and pays for airmail.

Best regards,
Your Seller

If the delay by the Postal Service was egregious, you might offer to sweeten the deal by refunding the shipping fee. If presented with this offer, a majority of buyers who respond say, "No refund is necessary. I have removed the comment." The customer has found a face-saving way to claim the moral high ground, and the feedback is removed.

Some buyers don't realize they can damage someone else's livelihood by leaving negative feedback. They seem to think the ratings are read by some anonymous person sitting in Amazon headquarters, and the matter ends there. Their realization that their (perhaps irresponsible) comment has been published on the Internet can prompt their cooperation in deleting it.

Problem customers. You need cooperation from buyers on removing inappropriate feedback because Amazon will rarely get involved in a dispute. The company's policy is to remove feedback only in two circumstances: when the feedback contains obscene language, and when it includes personal information such as your full name or telephone number.

Unfortunately, some buyers are just impossible to satisfy. Perhaps the buyer doesn't understand the feedback process, won't admit a mistake, or is just plain malicious. When all attempts to make amends fail, the important thing is to avoid taking it personally. Learn what you can from the experience and move on. Don't let a dispute with an unreasonable buyer distract you from running your business.

You can leave negative feedback for an Amazon buyer, but this accomplishes little beyond a momentary feeling of satisfaction for getting revenge. The buyer is probably unaware of feedback, and ratings from sellers don't count toward feedback averages anyway. This function can help you alert other sellers to a problem buyer, but what seller ever consults a buyer's feedback?

Feedback on other venues. Buyers on eBay and, to a lesser extent, its Half.com platform pay more attention to feedback etiquette. Feedback from sellers does count toward the overall average, but there is the option for "Mutual Feedback Withdrawal." When feedback is withdrawn, the positive, negative, or neutral rating associated with that feedback comment will no longer count toward your feedback score.

Delivery mistakes. Sometimes a Postal Service carrier scans a package "delivered" but fails to actually deliver it to the buyer's address. This can prompt a variety of reactions from your buyer. Here is a suggested script:

> *Dear [Customer],*
>
> *I'm sorry you haven't yet received the book. The tracking result means that the Postal Service carrier who walks your route scanned the package and indicated he/she left it at your address. I can think of a few possible explanations why you haven't received it:*
>
> *— The carrier left it at the wrong address and that person kept the package.*
>
> *— The package was stolen after delivery.*
>
> *— The carrier actually left the package on hold for you at the local post office but pressed the wrong button on his/her scanner and neglected to leave you a note indicating the package is at the post office.*
>
> *Is it possible for you to ask the carrier about this? That is the quickest way to resolve this. If the package can't be found, please let me know and I'll assist you in obtaining a refund from Amazon.*
>
> *Best Regards,*
> *Your Seller*

Your return policy. Decide on a return policy that you'll be able to explain consistently. In some cases, your return policy will be dictated by the selling platform on which you're participating. For example, Amazon Marketplace sellers are required to accept returns from customers postmarked within one week of receipt, with shipping costs paid by the buyer. That's the minimum requirement, but there's nothing to prevent you from having a more liberal policy.

You also need to comply with the federal mail order and telephone merchandise rule, also known as the "30-day rule" because it requires sellers to ship within the promised timeframe or within a maximum of 30 days. In cases where the advertised product can't be delivered, the law requires sellers to notify the customer and offer the option of a full refund within seven days.

Many successful sellers have a more liberal return policy, and a good rule of thumb is to treat customers the way you expect to be treated. When a customer wants to return an item for a reason you don't consider 100 percent legitimate, give the customer the benefit of the doubt. Your time is much better spent finding and listing books than trying to learn if a problem buyer is unethical or just stupid.

On the other hand, if you believe a buyer is definitely trying to pull a fast one, refer them to Amazon's A-to-Z program and let the customer plead their case to Amazon for a refund.

Selling used textbooks tends to create more than its share of disputes and returns. Student buyers can be particularly careless, assuming that just because they've found the correct title, they'll magically receive the correct edition too. Using this script, you can explain what went wrong, offer a solution, and avoid insulting the customer:

Dear Customer:

I'm sorry you cannot use the fourth edition text that I advertised and you purchased from me. I would be happy to refund you in full if you'll return the book within 30 days of receipt. I do not carry the fifth edition, but I have looked it up for you and you can locate a copy from a different seller at this link: [link].

I'm sorry this transaction didn't work out, but I did provide you with the book I advertised. For future reference, when you are looking for a specific edition of a text, it's best to search using the book's ISBN, a 10-digit code for your book that you can find by consulting your course syllabus or asking your instructor.

Best Regards,
Your Seller

Your Fulfillment System

We have seen how important it is to keep up with customer communications on a daily basis. That is the mental part of the selling process. Now we'll examine the physical aspect of the process, fulfilling orders.

Standardizing the way you handle customer orders will minimize mistakes and help you operate faster and more efficiently. Earlier we spoke of how small decisions on cost issues – obtaining the cheapest rates on postage and delivery confirmation – have a huge cumulative effect on your profitability.

Devising a routine way of storing, retrieving, and packing books for shipping can help you save a bit of time with each transaction and lead to a cumulative impact in *time* savings. And as we know, time is money.

Organizing inventory. New sellers typically organize their books in alphabetical order on a shelf. This works fine if your inventory consists of less than two dozen books, but when your inventory becomes several hundred books or more, alphabetizing becomes impractical. You'll have to reshuffle all the books – from A to Z -- each time you add new inventory, just to squeeze some into the middle.

Let's see how a simple SKU (stock keeping unit) system can simplify your daily chores. With an SKU system, we'll identify each book by a unique number, which we'll mark on the spine.

Let's suppose your books are stored on two bookshelves. We'll call them bookshelf A and bookshelf B. The SKUs for books on bookshelf A are A1, A2, A3, and so on. SKUs for books on the other bookshelf are B1, B2, B3, and so on.

Now, when you receive a "Sold, Ship Now" e-mail from Amazon, instead of picking through the alphabet to find the title, you'll grab the book by its SKU. Let's assume this method saves you 45 seconds each time you pull a book off the shelf for an order. As your business grows, those 45 seconds add up. Suppose your business expands to 80 orders a day. Multiply the 45 seconds 80 times daily, and you're saving one hour per day. Multiply that hour five days per week, 52 weeks a year, and you've saved 32 eight-hour days. That's 32 full workdays saved annually, just by using a simple SKU system.

And the SKU system saves time not only when we pull books *off* the shelf but also when we put new inventory *on* the shelf. Instead of hunting down the right spot in the alphabet and reshuffling all the books, you'll put the new books in the first available spot, giving it the appropriate SKU for its position on the shelf.

In case you're not sold on SKUs yet, here's another benefit: After your inventory is more than a few hundred books, you're likely to have multiple copies of some titles, each with a different condition and price. You don't want to accidentally send your "acceptable" copy to the customer who ordered the "like new" copy. If the two books have different SKUs, you won't make that mistake.

Designing your SKU system

Now that we have a concept for an SKU system, how do we actually put it into practice? How does the SKU get into your inventory listings and on the spine of the book?

If you're using Amazon's Inventory Loader to list new books, you'll notice a column for entering your SKUs. Third-party software like Seller Engine can generate a new SKU for each new book you list.

A simple way to affix the SKU to the spine of the book is to print the numbers on a sheet of removable Avery 5160 Labels. These small rectangular labels can be wrapped around the bottom of the book's spine so that the SKU is visible when you're facing the bookshelf. When you pick and pack the book, you can easily peel off the label, leaving no residue. (Be sure to use "removable" labels.)

You can write the SKUs on the labels by hand, or you can laser print the whole sheet of 30 at once. If you know how to use Microsoft Word form letters, you can mail-merge your list of new SKUs right onto the label sheet. You can download a free template to do this at www.avery.com

To learn how to use Amazon's Inventory Loader, consult the tutorial in Amazon's help section, http://www.amazon.com/exec/obidos/tg/browse/-

/1161312/. You can download an inventory template from Amazon by sending a blank e-mail to bulk-template-request@amazon.com.

Shipping

Decide on the type of shipping materials you'll use to mail your books. Three popular choices are cardboard boxes, corrugated bookfolds or b-flute, and bubble mailers. The type and value of the item being shipped can call for different materials. Padded or bubble envelopes may be fine for inexpensive paperbacks, but for more expensive books that need protection, use a box or bookfold that prevents bending and corner-bumping.

Stores like Staples and Office Depot have decent prices on shipping supplies, but you can save a good bit of money by buying shipping supplies in quantity through vendors like Associated Bag Co. and Uline. If you can get a cost savings of 20 cents for each bubble mailer, for example, that adds up to a fair amount of money over the year — which you can add to your bottom line. For a listing of several shipping vendors, see appendix 3 of this book.

If you've reached the point where you're shipping more than two packages a day, it's time to begin using an online postage service. Service fees are less than $8 a month, and the service allows you to avoid standing in line at the post office. Instead, you'll be able to prepare your shipments at your PC and drop off crates of your parcels at your post office's rear dock.

Tracking customers

When you reach the point that you're selling more than 10 books a day, your business will have too many moving parts for you to remember offhand. You'll begin receiving e-mails from buyers that seem to continue a conversation – except you don't know the conversation. Their e-mail doesn't include a copy of your original text, so there's no context. They'll say something vague like, "I really appreciate it — let me know!"

You might be tempted to reply, "Let you know WHAT? Who the hell are you?" But there's a more gracious way of handling this.

There are several free "desktop search" programs that can periodically index all the files on your computer's hard drive, including e-mails, shipping records, and spreadsheets. When you type in a buyer's name or e-mail address, for example, your desktop search program can instantly pull up all the files on your PC that contain that name — all your messages and records pertaining to that customer. No more rummaging around for 10 minutes to find some bit of information.

Here's an example of putting a desktop-search program to use: You get an "urgent" e-mail from Cool-Sam@net.com demanding to know, "Where is my Vonnegut book? I'm going on vacation in 10 minutes and I need it!" You search your payment transactions on Amazon's Web site, but there's no sale to Cool-Sam@net.com. So Sam is using a different e-mail address and it hasn't occurred to him to mention it, just like it hasn't occurred to him to mention the book title, his order number, or his last name. Again, you resist asking, "Who the hell are you?"

Instead, you type "Sam" and "Vonnegut" into your desktop search program. Instantly, his shipment confirmation e-mail pops up. You check the tracking and find out the book was delivered two weeks ago, case closed.

You can download desktop search programs from X1 (www.x1.com), Google (www.desktop.google.com) and Copernic (www.copernic.com/en/products/desktop-search). The Google and Copernic programs are free, and the Web portal Yahoo offers a free version of X1 that doesn't include all the functions of the paid version.

Collectible Books

The influx of new sellers into marketplaces like Amazon has driven down the prices of many commonly available books. The opposite has happened with collectible books, however, which have become scarcer and more expensive online, particularly in the past few years. For example, when Richard Russell updated his *Book Collector's Price Guide* in 2003, he reviewed the online prices for 120 classic rarities – books that command thousands of dollars, such as a first edition of *The Adventures of Tom Sawyer*. Just two years later, when Russell checked on those 120 classics again, he was surprised to find only 37 were still available online. Of the 37 still available, prices had appreciated dramatically on all but three titles, which fell modestly in price.

You could spend a lifetime and more learning about collectible books and how to sell them. If you're a regular seller, you'll start coming across some collectibles purely by accident. If you're interested in developing your business as a collectibles dealer, a good way to start is by picking a special area and focusing there. Your specialty should be whatever you have the most passion for — sports, business, cooking, the Civil War, computers, thrillers, romance, or whatever the subject area might be.

Today it's easier than ever to research collectible prices online. Before the Internet captured so much of the collectibles trade, dealing with collectible books required investing in an expensive, encyclopedic hard-copy publication such as *Bookman's Price Index* or *American Book Prices Current.* Today's new collector can get an introduction with *Official Price Guide to Books,* by Tedford and Goudey, now in its fifth edition, and Russell's *Antique Trader Book Collector's Price Guide,* mentioned above.

For the most current pricing information, search for the title on AddALL, at www.addall.com. An average of the prices listed there will give a good indication of the book's value, but price your copy at the high end of the range. Yes, you could choose to simply match the low price, but don't make a hasty decision on an item worth a substantial sum. Price high, and you can always revisit the decision later.

Why are prices rising for highly collectible books? For one thing, more people have become aware of collectibles, thanks to the Internet. On Amazon Marketplace, for example, the casual book buyer looking for a copy of Jane Austen's *Pride and Prejudice* sees not only that a used paperback copy is available for $1.48 but that there is a 1907 hardcover for $69.95. Collectible books are now being bought by an ever larger pool of consumers who just never thought about buying a rare book before.

Collectibles also go up simply due to supply and demand. There are a finite number of collectible books, and every day there are more buyers looking to buy them — a good recipe for price inflation. Expanded interest in regional collectible titles has also been attributed to the Internet. Specific titles about, say, Wyoming place names are now exposed to a worldwide pool of buyers. Banned books, self-published books, occult books — and just about any other kind of book one can imagine — become collectible if enough people are looking for it.

Certain types of collectible books are rising in price faster than others. The hottest titles today are those books that represent a "high spot" in a genre.

A few decades ago, collectors tended to map out their collection ahead of time using a rigid strategy. They would dutifully obtain a copy of each work by their favorite author, for example. Today, in-depth collections are out, and collections of the top 50 or 100 "trophy books" are in.

Collectors are zeroing in on those books deemed important or fashionable, the so-called high spots. As a result, prices for highly collectible books have appreciated faster than those of any other collectible category during the past 25 years. A novel adapted for a movie can become collectible overnight. Whether this focus on the high spots is driven by our media-saturated culture or the rise of the dilettante book collector is open to debate.

As they say in investing, past performance is no guarantee of future results, but consider this: if you had put $5,000 into high-spot books 20 years ago, you'd be worth a cool million today. To take but one example, Robert Chambers' 1939 *The Big Sleep* now goes for more than $12,500, largely because it was his first novel and the book was adapted for a movie. Even more recent books such as *The Catcher in the Rye* and *On the Road* are selling for more than $6,000.

For more on modern book collecting, read Brisbane's *Among the Gently Mad: Perspectives and Strategies for the Book Hunter in the 21st Century.*

Pricing. There may be many opinions on the value of a collectible, but when the rubber meets the road, the book is worth exactly what the buyer is willing to pay. The first step in your research should be to determine the current range of prices among competent sellers. The AddALL search engine, www.addall.com, will give you a good indication on the range of prices.

Newcomers to bookselling sometimes assume that older books are automatically more valuable than newer books, but nothing could be further from the truth. Automobiles don't instantly become collectible after they're 25 years old, and neither do books. What matters to book collectors is the author, the subject, the work's reputation, the book's condition, and how difficult a copy is to come by.

Condition. It's hard to overstate the importance of condition on the value of collectible books. Collectibles should have no serious defects, such as tears, soiling, foxing or writing. A missing dust jacket, for example, can knock 90 percent off the value of a collectible book, and library markings can knock a book out of the collectible category.

Modern first editions. Modern firsts (books produced within the past century) have become enormously popular among collectors during the past 15 years, and a huge variety of titles is available from which to acquire and sell. Prices have held up well, and these books are the bread and butter for many online collectible dealers.

By contrast, online values have deteriorated for so-called *hypermodern* firsts published in recent decades. Prices have been beaten down because of price competition among sellers and the plain fact that there are too many of these books. A first edition print run a couple of decades ago might have been 5,000 copies. By contrast, the 2005 installment of *Harry Potter* had an initial print run of more than 10 million copies. That volume means that first editions might be selling online for less than the paperback by the time the paperback comes out.

What to look for. Collectors who are looking for a "first edition" are actually looking for a "first printing." These are the books that roll off the presses when the book is released. They are collectible because they are scarcer and considered closest to the author's original inspiration. Some collectors use the term "first impression," which is synonymous with "first printing."

The initial print run for the vast majority of titles is small, under 10,000 copies — the smaller the first printing, the more valuable each book can become as a collectible. A popular book's first edition can span three dozen printings, while many books never go beyond the initial printing.

New booksellers will sometimes list a book as "collectible" and describe it as a "first edition, third printing." That description may be literally true, but a collector is not going to purchase the book.

Sometimes, the publisher will make changes to the book's text to fix typographical errors and other mistakes during a print run. The result is different "states" of the printing. Collectors are interested only in the first states of first printings.

How to recognize a first edition. Identifying a first edition can be tricky. Nearly every publisher has its own way to designate a first edition and later printings. To identify a printing, first look on the copyright page for a "statement of edition" or a number line. Sometimes the page states simply, "FIRST EDITION." Beware that publishers sometimes don't delete the words "FIRST EDITION" when they go on to the second printing, however.

Next, look for the number line, a sequence of digits that usually runs from 1 to 10 for a first edition. It may be in the usual sequence, or it may have the 1 on the left, the two on the right, and the 10 in the center. The main idea is to look for the 1, which every publisher uses to identify a first – every publisher except Random House, that is, which designates firsts with a 2 on the number line and the words "FIRST EDITION."

If you can't find a statement of edition or a statement of printing, look for a statement like the following: "First published in 1965." This statement is a good sign, because a publisher that indicates when the book was first published will indicate subsequent printings also. For older books, another way of determining edition is to compare the copyright page date with the title page date.

Also beware of book club editions. Sometimes the copyright page of a book club edition can read "FIRST

EDITION," but of course it isn't. You'll know it's a book club print by the absence of a price on the inside flap of the dust jacket. The inside of the dust jacket will often say "Book Club Edition" as well. After some experience handling books, you'll be able to spot a "book club" just by holding it in your hand. Club editions are somewhat smaller, made with cheaper materials, and lighter in weight than the original hardback. Many club editions also have an impression in the shape of a square or a circle on the bottom of the back cover.

All of this is not to say that a book must be a first edition to be collectible. Signed works, numbered editions, illustrated books, original paperbacks, and numerous other books may be collectible.

Collector's editions. Any discussion of collectible books must address so-called "collector's editions" made by outfits like Franklin Press, Easton Press, and Heritage. These are lovely books, often leather bound and finely made. They look great sitting on a shelf, but they're not really collectible. These books are sold new for about $40, and that is usually the most they are ever worth.

On the other hand, just because collectors don't take "collector's editions" seriously doesn't mean you can't resell them profitably. Franklin Press printings of classics like *The Adventures of Robinson Crusoe* and *The Young Lions* can be sold for $12 or so as a "collectible" on Amazon Marketplace, yet you can get them cheap by the box at some library sales.

Don't confuse this discussion of "collector's editions" with the pricier "limited editions," which are sometimes scarce enough that they become highly sought after and gain in value nicely after a few years.

Children's books. Children's books are one of the most popular areas for collectors, and as long as there are families, this trend will continue. Nostalgia buffs are always in the market for icons of their youth like *The Wonderful Wizard of Oz, Alice's Adventures in Wonderland, The Little Engine That Could*, and countless others.

The variety of formats in the children's category provides an opportunity for specialization in pop-ups, chapter books, picture books, and all the rest.

Science. It comes as a surprise to many new booksellers that the buying and selling of antiquarian science and medical texts is such an active market. The most sought-after items here are the first, groundbreaking works in a field — think Darwin's *Origin of Species*. As with fiction, these works represent the "high points" of a subject. Astronomy, physics, mathematics, chemistry, and rocketry are all active areas for collectors.

Advanced Automation

As noted at the outset, an online book business can start out simply, but it can quickly become a technical challenge as your inventory and sales volume grow and selling venues multiply. Fortunately, there have been a number of products and services introduced in the past few years to take some of the tedium out of the process.

As we've seen previously, shaving a bit of time on repetitive tasks can have a big cumulative effect. Depending on your business, some of the products listed here could provide the same kind of benefits by automating the manual tasks you perform from your PC. For example, with a broadband Internet connection and one of the price-checking tools listed below, you could review and adjust prices on 1,000 items in less than half an hour. Without automation tools, you might spend two or three days working at such a task.

Many of the tools made available for Amazon sellers have been developed by computer programmers who happened to be online booksellers themselves. It makes sense that sellers invented these products, since they are most familiar with the specific challenges of running an online book business.

Some third-party solution fees can be expensive, adding up to hundreds or thousands of dollars per year, but if a tool can double or triple your profitability, such costs may be justified.

If you're using a computer more than a few years old, you may need to upgrade to a more powerful machine to make full use of these tools. Some programs put a huge drain on your PC's processor, especially if you have a large inventory. If you haven't yet made the switch from dial-up service, a broadband Internet connection is also recommended.

Try the evaluation versions of software when they are available, and test the responsiveness of the company's technical support. If the company isn't responsive when you make an inquiry before purchasing, you can assume they will not be of great help after they've collected your money.

You should also consider the risk of leaving the proper functioning of your business operations at the mercy of a small entrepreneurial company. Your business can be damaged severely if your vendor's system goes haywire and can't be fixed promptly. For example, what would happen to your business if Amazon suddenly redesigned its system, and as a result, you could no longer use your vendor's software to manage inventory or print packing slips? If past history is any guide, you can count on this sort of thing happening a few times each year — so it's prudent to have a backup plan for how you'll operate when any of your vendors is down.

Some vendors faced with unexpected technical challenges have simply ceased operations, leaving their clients without service or refunds. In certain cases, payments may be recovered, but the larger issue is what happens to your business if it is held hostage to a service provider or piece of software that quits working.

If you're in the market for one of these services, check the vendor's Web site for testimonials from other reputable sellers. If you don't see any testimonials, ask the company for references. Any reputable company with a good product has no problem providing a list of happy clients.

Fees can add up quickly. Some vendors charge a modest one-time licensing fee for their software, but others want a cut of your monthly sales. If your monthly gross is just a few hundred dollars now, a fee of 3 percent in exchange for the use of a nifty service might seem fair. But what if your business expands to the point that your monthly gross is $10,000? Will you think that $300 a month, $3,600 a year, is fair for using that software? Many sellers believe a fee of more than 1 or 2 percent is excessive. At that rate, a high-volume seller could afford to hire a staff of computer programmers. Some question whether it's even legitimate for a service provider to ask for a percentage of a seller's fees when the service provider is not involved in the transactions.

Before you commit to a fancy automation tool, you might consider what type of automation tools you can build yourself. If you're fairly computer literate and can work with Microsoft Excel, you can devise your own method of automating order handling, for example. Using Amazon's downloadable fulfillment reports, you can use pre-built spreadsheets to generate packing lists and confirmation e-mails.

For sellers who would rather use pre-built software tools, here is a list of vendors who specialize in providing products for booksellers.

Pricing and inventory software

Seller Engine. www.sellerengine.com

Seller Engine was one of the first third-party software programs to make it easier for Amazon sellers to list new inventory and to check and adjust the prices on existing inventory. This PC software allows you to compare your prices with those of competing sellers without having to navigate to the Web page where your product is listed.

The program can also be used to research book prices. By importing a list of ISBNs, the program can help you decide which books are worth the most money on Amazon and worth your time to sell.

Fees. Users pay a monthly fee of $39.99. A free trial version of the software limits users to viewing 10 items at a time.

Bookrouter. www.bookrouter.com

Bookrouter enables booksellers to list their inventory on up to 19 online selling venues. Instead of having to upload inventory files to each site, Bookrouter automatically configures the data for each site. The service offers a way to adjust prices on different venues. You can raise or lower your prices by a percentage, a dollar amount, or a combination of those two factors on a site-by-site basis. Bookrouter also allows you to define a price range for books at various selling sites. It works with Amazon.com, ABAA/ILAB, Abebooks, Alibris, AntiQbook, Biblio.com, BiblioDirect, Bibliology, Biblion, Bibliophile, BookAvenue, Books&Collectibles, BookSellerSolutions, Choosebooks, Chrislands, Half.com, TomFolio, UsedBookCentral, and Wantedbooks.

Fees. Users pay $25 per month for up to five selling venues and $5 for each additional site. Bookrouter charges a one-time setup fee of $50, which covers listing on up to five selling venues — additional sites cost $5 each. The setup fee covers testing a sample upload and troubleshooting for each site.

Mail Extractor. www.mailextractor.com

Mail Extractor is an order fulfillment and inventory management program for booksellers using Amazon Marketplace and Half.com. The software resides on your PC. The program parses the information contained in Amazon order fulfillment reports and in Half.com and PayPal/eBay e-mails to build packing slips and invoices. Users can send automated e-mail shipment notifications to buyers and manage inventory. Mail Extractor also automates the printing of postage for users of the Endicia online postage service.

Fees. Users pay a monthly fee that depends on how many items they have listed for sale — starting at $6.95

for up to 1,500 listings and climbing to $44.95 a month for sellers with more than 30,000 listings.

AMan for Marketplace Sellers.

www.spaceware.com

AMan is an order fulfillment and inventory management software program designed for either low- or high-volume Amazon Marketplace and zShops sellers. It creates customized shipping labels, packing slips, and customer e-mails, as well as picklists for order fulfillment. AMan also exports customer addresses for online postage printing.

Fees. Users pay a one-time fee of $299. A 21-day free trial of the program is available.

BookHound. www.bibliopolis.com

The company Bibliopolis distributes BookHound, an inventory-management software tool for independent booksellers and dealers in antiquarian and out-of-print books. Based on the FileMaker Pro database engine, BookHound automates entering new stock, uploading inventory, and invoicing customers, among other tasks.

Fees. Use and technical support of BookHound costs $175 per year. A network version, BookHound Unleashed, is customized for each bookseller and its cost varies. The company has been selling BookHound for six years and says it has about 400 users.

Bibliopolis also offers database development and e-commerce and Web hosting services for independent booksellers. One example of an online bookstore hosted by Bibliopolis is Bray Books, www.braybooks.com.

HomeBase.
http://dogbert.abebooks.com/docs/homebase/main.sh tml

HomeBase is a free bookstore management software program distributed by Abebooks, a listing service for independent book dealers. It can be used to manage your inventory and issue receipts and invoices. The program is available for free download to anyone, regardless of membership in Abebooks.

PricePartner.
www.abebooks.com/docs/homebase/HB2PricePartner.s html

PricePartner is an application for users of Home-Base 2.0 and higher (see above) that allows you to quickly adjust prices of listed books.

FillZ. www.fillz.com

FillZ is an online inventory and order management system for Amazon booksellers with a high volume of sales. Users can upload their Amazon inventory to many additional bookselling sites. Inventory levels are adjusted automatically at each selling site. FillZ supports Amazon, eBay Stores, Abebooks, Alibris, and others.

You can add inventory using a bar code scanner or your existing software. Fulfillment functions include generation of picklists and packing slips by location, SKU number, and order number. The software also generates shipment confirmation e-mails and works with different online postage services.

Fees. There is a minimum monthly fee of $50 for sellers with under $3,000 in monthly sales. Sellers with between $3,000 and $10,000 in monthly revenue are charged the $50 minimum plus 1 percent of their monthly sales revenue over $3,000. Sellers with revenue over $10,000 in monthly revenue are charged a $120 monthly fee plus 0.5 percent of monthly revenue over $10,000. Shipping fees aren't included in calculating a seller's monthly revenue.

FillZ charges eBay sellers a flat monthly fee of $5 plus $2 for each thousand uploaded records, which includes new listings, updates, and deletions.

The Art of Books. www.theartofbooks.com

The Art of Books is an online service that enables booksellers to manage their inventory across several selling venues from a single interface. It includes tools to automate order fulfillment, postage printing, inventory repricing, and pricing information via cell phone. Supported venues include Amazon's U.S., Canadian, German, and U.K. sites; Alibris; Abebooks; and Half.com sellers with FTP accounts.

Fees. No fee is charged on the first $500 in monthly revenue, but users pay 1 percent of their monthly revenue between $500 and $10,000. A fee of 0.5 percent is paid on revenue over $10,000.

Prager Software. www.pragersoftware.com

Prager has a suite of PC software applications for inventory, pricing, and listing books on Amazon.

The inventory program enables sellers to upload to more than 18 bookselling sites and to generate customer invoices. The pricing program allows entry of up to 30 ISBNs at a time to retrieve pricing information, and a bar code scanner can be used to list inventory. Several options are available for adjusting prices, and Prager's listing synchronizer can be used to alert you to discrepancies in your inventory listings across different selling sites.

The programs are free. A licensing fee will be required for an enhanced version of the inventory program beginning in 2006.

Re-Price Machine. www.repricemachine.com

Doolicity Innovations makes software to help Amazon booksellers adjust their pricing and respond to customer e-mails.

The Re-Price Machine is a free program that enables sellers to automatically lower prices to match competitors. An upgraded version with more features is being planned that will require a fee.

Doolicity's Zipkeys is a data-entry tool that enables sellers to store customized responses to frequently asked questions from customers. Users can respond to certain e-mail inquiries with only one click.

Readerware. www.readerware.com

Readerware is a program for cataloging books, music, and video. The software has been used by collectors, booksellers, schools, churches, and libraries since 1999.

Fees. The basic version of the program costs $40. There's also a version for Palm handheld computers.

SellerMagic. www.sellermagic.com

Bordee Enterprises began promoting its Seller-Magic Amazon ListTool in late 2005. The software carries a strong resemblance to Seller Engine but has a few extra features. For example, when comparing your prices to competitors', Seller Magic enables you to put selected competitors into a separate group.

Fees. $24.95 a month.

ChannelAdvisor. www.channeladvisor.com

ChannelAdvisor Pro is an eBay auction management service designed for individuals and small businesses. The service helps you organize and track your inventory, and to create standardized auction listings. The service can also be used for eBay stores' fixed-priced listings.

Fees. ChannelAdvisor starts at $29.95 a month.

Feedback Assistant, Feedback Forager.
www.amazon.wolfire.com

Feedback Assistant automates the task of leaving feedback for your Amazon buyers. Feedback Forager automatically sends an e-mail to Amazon customers who haven't left a feedback rating and requests that they do so. The customer can rate the seller directly from the e-mail. This company also makes custom software for Amazon sellers.

Fees. One-time licensing fees are $20 for Feedback Assistant and $49.95 for Feedback Forager.

BookRepricer. www.bookrepricer.com

BookRepricer is an online service that compares your Amazon inventory with prices of competing sellers and then reprices your items automatically. Several options are supported for lowering and raising your prices. The company is based in the United Kingdom and supports Amazon's Marketplace platforms in the United States, the United Kingdom, and Canada.

Fees. Users pay a monthly subscription fee of $22 or an annual subscription fee of $180. A two-week free trial of the service is available.

BookSku. www.booksku.com

BookSku is an online service that enables Amazon sellers to automate the tasks of cataloging items, processing orders, printing packing slips, and connecting with online postage vendors. The service enables you to automatically reprice your inventory, track inventory locations, and send e-mails to customers, among other tasks.

Fees. Users pay $20 monthly for their first 500 listings, $2 per hundred listings between 500 and 5,000, and $1 per hundred listings over 5,000. The number of listings is calculated using an average from open listings reports.

Monsoon. www.monsoonworks.com

Monsoon began offering three levels of online service for booksellers in 2005. The service automates several processes, such as listing inventory, adjusting prices, and managing customers. The service supports sellers using Amazon Marketplace and six other bookselling venues. The company says its service can reprice up to 30,000 items per hour.

Fees. Monsoon asks that interested parties complete a signup form on their Web site because rates vary by the level of service a seller requires. Company representatives indicate that fees start at $199 for setup plus 3 percent of monthly sales.

BookWriter Web. www.bookwritersoftware.com

BookWriter Web is designed for booksellers who want to sell items on their own Web site. It automates the process of building Web pages to display your inventory. For booksellers who aren't interested in creating Web pages themselves, the company will customize a Web site for you for about $500.

Fees. Users pay a one-time licensing fee of $79 for BookWriter Web.

AZGrabber.

www.tuffcase.com/AZ/AZGrabber.htm

AZGrabber is a free Microsoft Excel spreadsheet that allows Amazon Marketplace sellers to generate a packing slip, shipping label, confirmation e-mail, and address file from Web pages in their seller account.

Fees. Tuffcase, the company that distributes AZ-Grabber, does not charge a fee but does solicit PayPal donations from active users.

Wireless pricing lookup

Many modern cell phones enable you to retrieve data over the Web. The services below enable you to check prices on Amazon Marketplace by inputting ISBNs or UPCs. The services can help you decide which books are worth adding to your inventory. Depending on your wireless device, you may be able to connect a bar code scanner and avoid having to key in the ISBNs. The services access Amazon's Web Services platform, so the data is retrieved much faster and with less clutter than browsing Amazon product pages.

ScoutPal. www.scoutpal.com

ScoutPal works with any Web-enabled cell phone or wireless PDA. You can also access prices from Amazon Marketplace, ABE, and PriceGrabber.com.

Fees. Users pay $9.95 monthly or $29.85 quarterly. A one-week free trial is available.

Bookhero. www.bookhero.com

Bookhero works with cell phones and wireless PDAs. It looks up pricing data on Amazon Marketplace. Up to 10 ISBNs can be retrieved in one request on a cell phone and up to 30 ISBNs on PDAs.

Fees. Users pay $8.95 monthly, $24.95 quarterly, or $89.95 annually.

AsellerTool. www.asellertool.com

AsellerTool looks up Amazon Marketplace prices for books, videos, and CDs using your cell phone, PDA, or PC. Users can retrieve data on up to nine items in one lookup operation. To keep waiting time to a minimum, the lookup result is limited to lowest used price, lowest new price, number of used listings, and the item's sales rank.

Fees. $4.99 a month. A seven-day free trial is available.

BookScout. www.theoldbookstore.com

This Web site operates a free cell phone lookup service. The company requires no fee but asks that you support it by purchasing items on Amazon.com through its referral link.

BookDabbler. www.bookdabbler.com

BookDabbler provides price and availability of new and used books at three levels of service, and offers a couple of options not available from other providers, including the ability to upload book wish lists.

Fees. Users pay a monthly fee of $5 to $9.95 depending on the service plan selected. A one-month free trial is available.

Online Postage

For sellers shipping more than a few packages a week, an online postage service can save tremendous amounts of time. Instead of waiting in line at the post office, then waiting for the clerk to apply postage to all your packages, you print the postage yourself in a fraction of the time.

Using online postage enhances your record keeping by automatically building a file of all your mailings right on your PC. Records on each parcel shipped can be retrieved in an instant — no rummaging through paper receipts required.

You can connect a digital scale to your PC to further automate the process. PC postage also allows you to purchase insurance and international postage when you need them.

Some online postage plans allow you to print "stealth postage," which does not print the dollar amount of postage on the address label, preventing customers from being irritated when the shipping and handling fee they paid is higher than the postage cost.

The established online postage vendors include:

Endicia. www.endicia.com

Endicia enables users to print U.S. postage on an envelope, label, or piece of paper from your laser printer.

If you're shipping more than a few dozen packages a day, consider adding a dedicated thermal label printer.

Endicia is easy for beginners to use to use but also has advanced capabilities for high-speed batch printing when needed.

Customer addresses can be imported from a database or copied from the clipboard. Users get free delivery confirmation on Priority Mail parcels. For Media Mail parcels, users get a discounted "electronic rate" of 13 cents per parcel for delivery confirmation, compared to the "retail" fee of 50 cents you'll pay at the post office.

Endicia also enables users to purchase insurance from U-Pic Insurance Services, which offers more competitive rates than the Postal Service.

Fees. Users pay $9.95 monthly or $99.95 annually for the basic plan, and $15.95 monthly or $174.95 annually for premium service. A 30-day free trial is available. The premium service includes more automation capabilities and the ability to print "stealth" postage.

Stamps.com.   www.stamps.com

Stamps.com's online postage service is similar to Endicia's but does not have the same range of features and support. Users can print stealth postage.

Fees. Users pay $15.99 monthly.

Shipstream Manager.

www.pitneyworks.com/shipstream

Shipstream is offered by Pitney Bowes, which used to be a popular source from which to rent postage meters. The recently introduced Shipstream is its first Internet postage product that has the range of features required for businesses shipping parcels.

Fees. Users pay $18.99 monthly.

eBay/PayPal.

PayPal and eBay users can print address labels that include postage for buyers using PayPal. No Postal Service account registration or software installation is needed. Stealth postage and insurance are available, as are pre-populated address fields.

Fees. There is no monthly fee, but a processing fee of 20 cents is charged for each Media Mail, First Class, or Parcel Post label printed. There's no fee for Priority Mail or Express Mail labels.

Click-N-Ship.

www.usps.com/shipping/label.htm

The U.S. Postal Service enables online users to print shipping labels at this site. Registration is required for postage and batch label orders. At this time, postage may be printed only for Express Mail and Priority Mail labels.

USPS Shipping Assistant.

www.usps.com/shippingassistant

This free PC-based software distributed by the U.S. Postal Service creates shipping labels with delivery confirmation, signature confirmation, or Express Mail service. Users can receive discounted rates for Delivery Confirmation and Signature confirmation, and can calculate rates and send customers e-mail notification that the package is on the way, including the delivery confirmation number. Users must pay for postage separately.

Shipwire. www.shipwire.com

Shipwire is a free service that enables users to compare rates from the Postal Service, UPS, and three other carriers. Users can print shipping labels and schedule pickups. Freight providers are also listed for heavier shipments. The company has a store for packaging materials at shipwire.com/exec/d_packaging.php.

Other resources

The Postal Service, UPS, and other carriers maintain several online resources that can help assess shipping options.

Domestic Rate Calculators.

USPS:

http://www.usps.com/tools/calculatepostage

UPS:

ww.ups.com/using/services/rave/rate.html

International Rate Calculators.

International shippers may wish to consult these resources:

USPS: http://ircalc.usps.gov/

UPS:
www.ups.com/using/services/rave/rate.html

DHL: www.dhl-usa.com/shipping/

FedEx: www.fedex.com/us/international

Taxes, Legal Requirements, and Records

If you're running a business, you need good records to prepare your tax returns. These records must support the income, expenses, and credits you report on your return. Generally, these are the same records you use to monitor your business and prepare your financial statements.

Business records must be available in case the IRS demands an inspection at any time. If the IRS asks for an explanation of your tax returns, complete records will help conclude the examination quickly.

In addition to staying on the right side of the law, keeping good business records will help you manage your business more effectively through these critical tasks:

- **Monitoring your business's progress.** Records will show whether your business is improving or faltering, where sales are coming from, and what changes in your practices you might need to make. Good records give you a better chance of making your business succeed.

- **Preparing financial statements.** Good records are essential for preparing accurate financial statements. These statements can aid in any necessary dealings with your bank and creditors, as well as help you make business decisions.

- **Identifying receipt sources.** Your business will have money and goods coming in from various sources, and you'll need to keep this information separate from personal receipts and other income.

Your business's legal structure

Once you've decided to pursue bookselling as a regular endeavor, you'll need to decide how your business will be formally organized and how you'll meet your tax obligations. As your business grows, you should periodically revisit the question of what the best form of organization is for your business.

Sole proprietorship. Establishing a sole proprietorship is cheap and relatively simple. This term designates an unincorporated business that is owned by one individual, the simplest form of business organization to start and maintain. You are the sole owner and you take on all the business's liabilities and risks. You state the income and expenses of the business on your own tax return.

Any business that hasn't incorporated is automatically a sole proprietorship. So if you haven't incorporated, formed a partnership, or established a limited liability company, your business is a sole proprietorship by default.

The good news about a sole proprietorship is that you're entitled to all the profits from the business. On the other hand, you are 100 percent responsible for all debts and liabilities. So if your business is sued, your personal assets could be seized.

As a sole proprietorship, you're liable for paying income tax and self-employment tax (Social Security and Medicare taxes), and for filing quarterly estimated taxes based on your net income. Since you don't have an employer reporting your income and withholding a portion of your paycheck for taxes, you must inform the IRS about the income from your bookselling and make quarterly tax payments on the profits. Quarterly installments of the estimated tax, submitted with Form 1040-ES, are due April 15, June 15, September 15, and January 15 of the following calendar year. If you don't yet sell full-time and you also work at a job where your employer withholds income for taxes, you can ask your employer to increase your withholding. That way you can avoid having to mail in quarterly estimated payments on your book profits.

As far as the IRS is concerned, a sole proprietorship and its owner are treated as a single entity. Business income and losses are reported with your personal tax return on Form 1040, Schedule C, "Profit or Loss From Business."

If you've never filed a Schedule C with the IRS before, you may wish to hire an accountant to assist you with the first year's return. The following year you may want to complete the return yourself. Another option is to use tax-preparation software such as TurboTax to complete your return. Unlike the IRS instruction pamphlets, TurboTax guides you through the process in plain English. The program can save you several hours at tax time because you don't have to decipher the IRS's language.

Partnership. A partnership is the relationship between two or more persons who agree to operate a business. Each person contributes something toward the business and has a stake in its profits and losses. Partnerships must file an annual information return to report the income and deductions from operations. Instead of paying income tax, the partnership "passes through" profits or losses to the partners, and each partner includes their share of the income or loss on their tax return.

Corporation. In a corporation, prospective shareholders exchange money or property for the corporation's stock. The corporation generally takes deductions similar to those of a sole proprietorship to calculate income and taxes. Corporations may also take special deductions.

Limited liability company. A limited liability company (LLC) is a relatively new business structure allowed by state statute. LLCs are popular because owners have limited personal liability for the company's debts and actions, as is also the case for a corporation.

Local ordinances

Call your county government headquarters to ask what types of permits and licenses are required for your business. Some cities, counties, and states require any business to get a business license. If you're working at home, your city or county may require a "home occupation permit" or a zoning variance, and you may have to certify that you won't have walk-in retail customers. Since your business is an online and mail-order business, this shouldn't be a restriction.

If you are conducting your business under a trade name such as "YourBookPeddler," you should file a "fictitious name" certificate with your county or state government office so people who deal with your business can find out who the legal owner is. This is also known as a DBA name (Doing Business As) or an "assumed name."

Sales taxes. Although the Internet is a "tax-free zone" in many respects, this does not apply to state sales taxes for goods sold to customers in your state. To pay the tax, you'll need to open an account and obtain a "resale license," known as a resale number or sales tax certificate in some instances.

You don't collect state sales tax on orders shipped outside your state, however. This is because Internet sales — as well as fax, telephone, and mail-order sales — shipped to another state aren't subject to sales tax unless you have an office or warehouse located there. In some states, shipping and handling fees are not subject to sales tax, but in some they are — you will need to investigate the issue for your home state.

Once you've made the decision that your bookselling is no longer a hobby, obtain a resale certificate from your state tax office. This will relieve you of paying state sales tax on the items you buy for resale, but it will also obligate you to report and pay taxes on the sales you make to customers within your state. The resale certificate will entitle you to a 10 percent "dealer's discount" at most bookshops, and some offer up to 20 percent off.

Income taxes. Your form of business determines which income tax return form you have to file. For the vast majority of booksellers without employees or a walk-in store, a sole proprietorship makes the most sense. As noted previously, the other most common forms of business are partnerships, corporations, and limited liability companies.

Many persons starting their own part-time business spend lots of time thinking about what they'll be able to write off on their tax return, but it is better to think of this exercise as paying taxes on your net profits. Your write-offs are the costs of doing business, such as buying books and paying for postage. What's left over is the profit, and you pay income tax on it. As far as the IRS is concerned, your business must become profitable within three years or it will be considered a hobby, and none of the expenses will be deductible.

For example, your mileage traveling to book sales is deductible for tax purposes. Don't rely on your memory to keep track of such expenses. Keep a notebook in your car to document the mileage and expenses for your buying trips. If you're ever audited by the Internal Revenue Service, the IRS will want to see documentation for your travel and other deducted expenses.

To figure your taxes, you'll need to keep track of every transaction involving your book business. Keep receipts and records, and put your expenses into categories such as "postage," "shipping supplies," "books," and so on.

Your bookkeeping chores can be greatly simplified with financial software such as Quicken. Most banks offer free downloads of your transactions, and once you set it up, Quicken can automatically categorize all your business expenses and eliminate most of the headaches at tax time. If you have a debit or check card linked to your account, you can use the card for nearly all your business transactions. Those records can be downloaded into Quicken right along with your banking records, making your bookkeeping that much simpler.

Supporting documents. The law doesn't require any particular record keeping technique, as long as you can plainly show your income and expenses. Your records must summarize your business transactions, showing your gross income, deductions, and credits. It's a good idea to have a separate checking account for your business so that your personal funds are not included.

You should preserve the paper trail of any purchases, sales, and other transactions, including any invoices or receipts, sales slips, bills, deposit slips, and records of canceled checks. Keep these documents that support your tax return organized and in a secure place. More detailed information is available in IRS Publication 583, "Starting a Business and Keeping Records."

Business use of your home

You may be able to deduct expenses related to the business use of parts of your home. This deduction is subject to certain requirements and doesn't include expenses such as mortgage interest and real estate taxes.

To qualify to claim expenses for business use of your home, you must use part of your home exclusively and regularly as your principal place of business or for storage. This means the area used for your business must be a room or other separate identifiable space, but you are not required to designate the space by a permanent wall or partition.

There are some exceptions to the "exclusive use" test. If you use part of your home for storage of inventory, you can claim expenses for the business use of your home without meeting the exclusive use test — but you must meet these criteria:

- Your business is selling wholesale or retail products.
- You keep the inventory in your home for use in your business.
- Your home is your business's only fixed location.
- You use the storage space on a regular basis.
- The space used for storage is a separately identifiable space suitable for storage.

To qualify under the regular use test, you must use a specific area of your home for business on a regular basis. "Incidental" or "occasional" business use is not regular use as far as the IRS is concerned.

Insurance. Home-based businesses aren't usually covered under a regular homeowners or renter's insurance policy. If your books are stolen or damaged, it's probably not covered. If a delivery person or customer is injured at your home, you may be liable unless an "endorsement" or "rider" is added to your homeowner's or renter's policy. The cost of the additional premium is usually quite low for a business without employees or a huge inventory.

Bookkeeping. For a small bookselling business, simple "cash basis" bookkeeping should suffice. The cash method entails recording income when money is received and expenses as they are paid. "Cash basis" does not necessarily mean your transactions are in cash, but refers to checks, money orders, and electronic payments as well as currency. If you're not familiar with the basics of bookkeeping, read *Small Time Operator: How to Start Your Own Business, Keep Your Books, Pay Your Taxes and Stay Out of Trouble* by Bernard Kamoroff.

Cash accounting is simpler to understand and use than the other type of bookkeeping, accrual accounting. Businesses are allowed to use cash accounting if annual sales are below $1 million.

Hiring employees. The decision to begin hiring employees is a big step for any business. Although employees can enable you to expand your activities and profits, hiring will add tremendously to your paperwork and the extent to which your business is regulated by the government. Having employees means that you need to keep payroll records and withhold income, Social Security, and state taxes, as well as Medicare and worker's compensation insurance. The states and the IRS require timely payroll tax returns and strict observance of employment laws. Penalties are usually swift and severe for failure to pay payroll taxes.

An entrepreneur might be tempted to pay cash "under the table" for help instead of hiring employees during their transition from a one-person shop to employer status. There is no gray area here — such practices are illegal because payroll taxes and worker's compensation insurance aren't being paid.

An alternative to taking on employees is to hire an independent outside contractor. You can hire contractors as needed, and the practice entails less paperwork and none of the headaches of paying employment taxes or producing payroll tax returns.

If you hire an independent contractor, make certain the person doing the work understands completely that they are not an employee. Numerous small business owners have gotten into scrapes with state and federal regulators when their independent contractors were later denied unemployment compensation or were found not to have paid their own Social Security taxes.

The Future of Bookselling

We've seen how the Internet has revolutionized the book trade by introducing millions of consumers to used, out-of-print, and collectible books. This has been a boon for publishers and readers alike. Tens of thousands of obscure titles have become available again, indeed been discovered again, and some have even come back into print because of the new demand flowing from readers searching on the Internet.

The next decade is going to be a bumpy ride for booksellers, however. So far, the impact of downloadable electronic books has been minimal, and no wonder. The big publishers have refused to discount them much, giving consumers little incentive to buy. When a book buyer has a choice between a fancy hardcover for $15 and an e-book for $13.59, she's choosing the hardcover.

Although its rival, Barnes & Noble, killed off its e-book program in 2003 citing lack of demand, Amazon seems increasingly interested in e-books. However, the bickering over e-books totally ignores the fact that free nonfiction content on the Web has already made entire book categories obsolete. Nobody predicted 15 years ago that the hard-copy encyclopedia business would virtually disappear. Now the question is how fast this might extend to lower-priced dictionaries, almanacs, and other types of books.

Meanwhile, a new printing technology has already changed the economics of niche titles. Print-on-demand (POD) enables publishers to efficiently print single copies of books for which there has not been enough demand for a new edition. In the future, it's possible that no title would ever have to go out of print. A book could simply be printed each time a customer orders one. This could reduce the value of scarce used books and shrink the territory for sellers specializing in of out-of-print books.

Publishers already have nearly all books published within the past 15 to 20 years in an electronic format, which facilitates this new technology. But it's unclear whether POD would be profitable enough to pay for scanning and inputting older titles for which no electronic file exists.

What will this mean for booksellers? Today it's practical for the largest brick-and-mortar shops to carry only 3 percent of the titles that have ever been produced since bookmaking began. A decade from now, bookstores may be able to instantly print just about any book a customer might be seeking.

Amazon.com itself bought out one of the leading POD companies, BookSurge, in 2005, and it will be interesting to see how Amazon might use BookSurge to print books for customers. BookSurge could also help Amazon capture part of the rapidly expanding pool of self-publishing authors who want to outsource their book production and marketing.

A proliferation of sales venues. There are dozens of players in the online book market today. Amazon practically has a monopoly in terms of volume, but the pendulum may start swinging back before long. As growing numbers of consumers become comfortable with online shopping, new competition will likely threaten Amazon's dominant perch as a Web platform for new and used book sales.

One fear of online sellers has always been that a few big portals — such as Amazon, eBay, and Yahoo — would control all online trading. That looks less likely now than ever. Bookselling sites are beginning to pop up on the Web on a regular basis, and sellers with just a few thousand books are starting to operate their own Web stores.

Google

The search firm Google is testing a Web marketplace, Froogle, which may become a huge sales venue if for no other reason than Google's inordinate influence over Internet traffic. Google is also developing a "wallet" payment system that would allow it to collect funds for sellers much as PayPal has automated payments on eBay.

Most importantly, Google is busily adding the full text of every book it can get its hands on to its database, which enables the search-engine giant to display book titles and sample pages when relevant to a user's search. Currently, Google is probably sending 90 percent of book buyers to Amazon. If it began sending buyers only to Froogle, eBay, or somewhere else, this could put a huge dent in Amazon's business.

Some booksellers have already been experimenting with Adwords, the Google program in which advertisers pay to display relevant text ads on millions of Web sites. Booksellers haven't had much success with Adwords, since they don't have the profit margins to pay much for getting a buyer to click through to their site.

For the foreseeable future, it's clear that the Internet will have a growing and rapidly evolving influence on how consumers discover and purchase books. Booksellers will need to adapt quickly to those changes or risk becoming obsolete.

Opening a brick-and-mortar shop

After launching a successful online book business, some sellers can't resist the dream of opening a physical store, and there is one advantage: you wouldn't need to leave the store to acquire new stock – customers could bring new inventory in for trades. The negative about a physical store is that you become chained to it and must keep it open during regular daytime and evening business hours.

Many former brick-and-mortar shop owners who now sell only online say they can't think of a single good reason for opening the physical store up again, and they point to these drawbacks:

- You'll need to physically organize your books by subject and author, which isn't required for Internet selling, and you'll need to reorganize books each time they are disorganized by browsing customers.

- It's hard to find qualified, knowledgeable employees to work in a used bookshop.

- Evenings and weekends off will be few and far between.

- It will be a challenge to pay the rent at a location with adequate foot traffic for a bookstore. (Owning the building is often a better option.)

- You'll need to purchase expensive liability insurance in case a customer slips on your sidewalk and sues.

And here are some additional headaches you'll have with a brick-and-mortar store:

- Shoplifters.

- Paying for unemployment insurance.

- Employee theft.

- Collecting sales taxes on all walk-in sales.

- Advertising expenses. A one-eighth page ad in the Yellow Pages in a medium-sized market can cost $400 per month. If there's a used or antiquarian book association in your region, join it and get listed in their advertising or brochures if possible. Alternative, free, and weekly newspapers are good advertising channels.

Many owners of used bookshops try to keep costs down by cramming a lot of inventory into a small building in a bad part of town. That type of operation doesn't cut it with most shoppers these days, and size and selection are more important than ever. In years past, many small used bookshops did well with inventories of 10,000 to 20,000 books. But many experts believe that an inventory of 80,000 to 100,000 books is required to get the critical mass of consumers through your doors today.

If you're still interested in opening a small used bookstore but aren't quite sure how to go about it, you can check into franchising opportunities with the Little Professor chain of stores.

See www.littleprofessor.com/franchise.html.

Appendix 1
Remainder Book Wholesalers

Remainder book wholesalers sell relatively recent titles, often at 75 to 85 percent off the retail price. All of the vendors listed here offer ordering over the Internet and will ship anywhere in the United States, usually via UPS or freight truck. Most vendors require a minimum order of $100 to $300, and an application for a new account must be accompanied by a copy of your state sales tax exemption certificate, which indicates that you pay state sales tax on the shipments you make to customers in your state. Some vendors require prepayment of the first order, with future orders to be paid in 30 days. However, it is becoming increasingly common for vendors to require prepayment via credit card on all orders.

Limit your risk with remainders by sticking with titles that have a solid track record of positive book reviews from readers on Amazon.com. Many current best-sellers have awful reviews from readers who were disappointed after purchasing the book. These are the books that remainder distributors will have in good supply because bookstore chains are returning them, and their online price will sink rapidly.

First editions are often remaindered, and astute booksellers will snatch up the titles by name-brand authors and store them for a year or two. After other sellers compete with each other to sell these titles at 50 percent to 75 percent off retail, exhausting the supply of remainders, it's possible to sell these titles at the original full retail price or even higher, depending on the popularity of the author.

The last quarter of the calendar year is a good time to buy remainder stock. Dealers are flush with the previous year's hot sellers and ready to make room for next year's.

Don't be shocked if prices on your remainder titles plunge for a while. Several other remainder sellers probably have gotten the same title at about the same time and have begun a race to the bottom in a contest to sell out first.

If prices go too low for your liking, wait out the lowballers. Eventually they'll exhaust their supply of remainders and you can resume selling at a higher price. But there's no guarantee you'll be able to sell all your remainder titles profitably. If you buy enough remaindered titles you're bound to end up with some losers.

So getting into remainders is a whole lot riskier than selling one-of-a-kind used books. Unlike library sales, where you can pick winners blindfolded, as noted previously, you can't go on hunches to buy remainders or you'll lose money. Buy only those titles that still sell for most of their cover price and have steady sales according to Amazon sales rank.

Describing remainders. It's an open debate whether remainders can honestly be described as "new" or must be called "used." Certainly, however, if a book is in perfect condition and has never been handled since it rolled off the printing press, it can be described as "new" whether it's been remaindered or not.

One hazard of remainder stock is the "remainder mark," usually a line drawn in black marker on the bottom edge of the pages. The mark is drawn so that the publisher won't have to accept returns of these books at the retail price. Some publishers use a fancy stamp or a small red dot to be less conspicuous. In any case, you should fully disclose and describe remainder marks in your online listing.

How much the remainder mark detracts from the value of the book depends on the type of remainder mark and the book. Most buyers who just want to read an inexpensive book will not notice or care about a remainder mark. By contrast, however, remainder marks are a big concern for book collectors.

Remainder stores. Retail bookstores specializing in publisher overstocks are becoming more popular, but the vast majority of the stock in these stores will be unsuitable for used booksellers because it's too plentiful online and prices will be low. But it is possible to find some good deals. The stock turns over fast at these types of venues, so check back often. It is possible to pick up some signed first editions and limited editions at remainder stores.

More information on the remainder market and vendors is available in the online publication "Bargain Book News," www.imakenews.com/BargainBookNews.

A list of 24 reputable remainder dealers follows:

A1 Overstock
Netcong, NJ
www.a1overstock.com
info@a1overstock.com
973-426-9997
A wide assortment of remainders and hurts (new books that have suffered some cosmetic damage) in all categories. New titles are added every day. Order individual titles or skids of assorted titles.

American Book Company
www.americanbookco.com
bburtner@americanbookco.com
Knoxville, TN
865-966-7454
Remainder and overstock books, including hardcover fiction and nonfiction, children's, cookbooks, coffee-table books, audio, trade formats, and hurt skids. This company has associations with Penguin Putnam, Harper Collins, Abrams, and Brilliance Audio.

Bargain Books Wholesale
Grand Rapids, MI
www.bargainbookswholesale.com
Debbiesmith@bargainbookswholesale.com
717-227-9576

Remainders, hurts, and closeout books. A variety of categories, with emphasis on children's books, cookbooks, collectibles, crafts, home improvement, inspirational, religion, and transportation.

Book Depot
Thorold, Ontario, Canada
www.bookdepot.com
rick@bookdepot.com
905-680-7230
Perhaps the widest selection of any remainder distributor, within tens of thousands of titles. Books in all categories, including fiction, nonfiction, children's, audio, and religion. Order through the Web site or at the warehouse.

Book Sales, Inc.
New York, NY
www.booksalesusa.com
sales@booksalesusa.com
866-483-5456
A publisher and supplier to booksellers of other publishers' overstock and remainder titles for resale.

BooksNSave
Phoenix, AZ
www.booksnsave.com
vasantabhyanker@hotmail.com

602-957-0956

Specializes in computer, medical, technology, educational, and miscellaneous books in categories such as coffee-table books and cookbooks. All books are brand new; a few may have a remainder mark from the publisher.

Bradley's Book Clearance
Pittsburgh, PA
sales@bradleysbooks.net
www.bradleysbooks.net
412-243-6637

A bargain book wholesaler dealing in current hardcovers, paperbacks, and mass market books. Specializes in African-American, history, mass market, and new age. Also carries book-related items such as journals, diaries, bookmarks, book covers and magazines.

Daedalus Books
Columbia, MD
pnuhn@daedalusbooks.com
www.daedalusbooks.com
800-333-5489

Remainders in every subject, including the arts, children, history, house and home, nature, and science. Also carries music, specializing in jazz, blues, world, classical, and opera. Wholesale discount requires minimum $200 purchase.

East Tennessee Trade Group
Madisonville, TN
larry@rhinosales.com
www.rhinosales.com
423-442-3693
Specializing in children's, cooking, craft, and home improvement books. Also carries large assortments loaded onto pallets.

Fairmount Books, Inc.
Buffalo, NY
www.fairmountbooks.com
psnow@fairmountbooks.com
905-475-0988
Remainders and publishers' overstocks. More than 4,000 titles on all subjects, including children's books, fiction, cooking, gardening, reference, history, and health.

Great Jones Books
Millwood, NY
www.greatjonesbooks.com
sales@greatjonesbooks.com
914-762-6562
More than 3,000 titles in literature, history, art, architecture, philosophy, social sciences, and more. Now carries a selection of general-interest trade books and children's books. New titles added weekly.

J R Trading Company
Monmouth Junction, NJ
www.jrtradingco.com
deb@jrtradingco.com
732-329-3500
Remainders, returns, and bargain books. No inventory catalog is published, but the company sends an email and fax inventory list when available.

Kudzu Book Traders
Cartersville, GA
www.kudzubooks.com
books@kudzubooktraders.com
770-607-8790
Discount wholesaler representing all major publishers. Deals in all categories of remainders, overstocks, and hurt skids. No minimum order.

LRA Books
New York, N.Y.
www.lrabooks.com
customerservice@lrabooks.com
917-779-8790
Independent distributor of individual and large book lots. Specializes in nonfiction books, especially history and social science.

Marketing Resource
New York, NY
212-447-7100
www.mribargains.com
mavedis@mribargains.com

More than 2,500 remainder and overstock titles. Subjects include children's books, gardening, cooking, art, travel, crafts, history, biography, reference and Christian books. Also carries stationery and related closeout items.

Maximus Books, LLC
Tannersville, PA
www.maximusbooks.com
sforsell@maximusbooks.com
570-619-8004

Discount books including remainders, hurts, and select promotional titles from all publishers. Showroom visits available in Tannersville by appointment

Reader's World USA, Ltd.
Oakland, OH
www.readersworldusa.com
inquiry@readersworldusa.com
732-240-3018

Wholesale supplier of books and general merchandise with over 5,000 remainder titles in stock.

S & L Sales Company, Inc.
Waycross, GA
www.slsales.com
jim@slsales.com
800-243-3699
Remainder wholesaler of adult fiction, nonfiction, and children's books. No minimum order.

Strictly By The Book
Fall River, MA
www.strictlybythebook.com
CustomerService@StrictlyByTheBook.com
508-675-5287
Wide selection, including more than 10,000 children's titles. Customers can also shop at the Fall River, MA, warehouse. Minimum order is $200 and quantity of three per title.

Tartan Book Sales
Williamsport, PA
www.tartanbooks.com
tsteinbacher@brodart.com
800-233-8467 ext. 6789
A division of the Brodart library supply company, Tartan offers recycled library edition hardcovers. Bestsellers and other popular titles are available by the title or in bulk. Shipping for small orders is $2.20 for the first

book and $.75 for each additional book, with special rates for bulk orders.

WGP Distribution Co., Inc.
Ardmore, PA
www.wgpbooks.com
ira@wgpdist.com
610-642-6420

A remainder, hurt, and closeout wholesaler. Categories include coffee-table, gardening, cooking, children's, how-to, self-help, religious and psychotherapy, craft, military, Civil War, and selections of fiction and nonfiction.

Warehouse Books, Inc.
Norfolk, VA
www.warehousebooksinc.com
marie@warehousebooksinc.com
757-627-4160

General categories, including children's, cooking, crafts, and military. Some music remainders, including sheet music, CDs, cassettes, VHS, and more.

West Coast Bargain Books
Bellingham, WA
www.wcbbooks.com
mitch@wcbbooks.com
360-671-9828

Sells general and computer books by the title or by assortment. Carries regional titles, cookbooks, children's, how-to, fiction.

World Publications, Inc.
North Dighton, MA
www.wrldpub.net
salesdept@wrldpub.net
508-880-5555
Remainder and promotional books in all genres except textbooks and mass market.

Appendix 2
New Book Wholesalers

New books. Selling new books in an Internet marketplace is a tough, low-margin business due to aggressive discounting by Amazon of 30 to 40 percent for popular titles in recent years. Normally the biggest discount you'll be able to get on new books from a wholesaler is around 45 percent. That leaves little room to cover costs like returns, lost packages, damaged books, and other mishaps.

But this business model can work, and there are several sellers who sell thousands of the latest bestsellers right on Amazon Marketplace, just a few cents under Amazon's price. Of course Amazon gets the vast majority of the sales, because of their name brand and free shipping offers. But some buyers will choose the Marketplace seller for a single item, since standard Marketplace shipping is $3.49, versus $3.99 from Amazon.

With such a small profit margin on the top bestsellers, some sellers of new books opt not to compete with the most popular bestsellers. Instead, these sellers search for steady sellers in the 100,000 Amazon sales rank range that are not heavily discounted.

Unfortunately several Amazon Marketplace vendors have been known to "game" the system, selling without actually having the books on hand. Only after the customer orders does the seller place an order with his wholesaler. This leads to shipping delays at best, and as a result the feedback ratings of these sellers are usually horrible. These sellers cancel many Marketplace orders when the book becomes unavailable through their wholesaler, which irritates customers and casts a pall on the online shopping experience. Sellers advertising an item for sale should have it on hand for immediate shipment.

The following is a listing of new book wholesalers who service retailers.

Ingram Book Co., www.ingrambookgroup.com, of Nashville, is the largest U.S. wholesaler to independent book dealers, serving about 9,000 retailers, including Amazon itself. With five regional warehouses, Ingram manages next-day delivery to nearly every address in the United States.

If you want to expand your sales potential by adding new books to your inventory, your first step should be to call an Ingram representative at 800-937-0152. The company will want to know if bookselling is your primary business. If so, you may be eligible to establish an account. If not, it would be necessary for you to purchase at least $5,000 in inventory annually. Initial orders must be for at least 100 books or a wholesale value of $500 or more.

To be eligible for an account with Ingram or most other wholesalers you will need to provide your resale certificate or tax exemption certificate number, which you should obtain from your state's tax department.

If more than half of your offerings are Christian books, Ingram will probably want to refer you to its Spring Arbor Distributors unit, which can be accessed on the Web at www.springarbor.com or by telephone at 800-395-5599.

Baker & Taylor, www.btol.com, of Bridgewater, NJ, is the primary alternative to Ingram. Baker & Taylor carries more titles than Ingram, but is more oriented toward schools and libraries. Baker and Taylor can be reached at 800-775-1800.

The other major book wholesalers serving U.S. booksellers, some of which limit their trade to mass-market paperbacks and other specialties, include:

Ambassador Book Service, Hempstead, NY
800-431-8913
www.absbook.com

Blackwell's Book Services, Blackwood, NJ
800-257-7341
www.blackwell.com

Bookazine Corp., Bayonne, NJ
800-221-8112
www.bookazine.com

DeVorss and Company, Marina del Rey, CA
800-772-4304
www.devorss.com

The distributors, South Bend, IN

800-348-5200
www.thedistributors.com

Sunbelt Publications, El Cajon, CA
800-626-6579
www.sunbeltpub.com

Appendix 3
Shipping Supply Vendors

The first two vendors listed here, Associated Bag and Uline, can handle needs for most shipping materials such as boxes, tape, mailers and labels. These are established, reliable companies that offer excellent service. You can sometimes obtain unique items and special deals from the other vendors listed below. If you can find a vendor in your area, you may be able to arrange a pickup and save the freight charges, so check your local Yellow Pages for additional sources.

Associated Bag Co.   www.associatedbag.com

Associated Bag has a huge selection of nearly every type of shipping material made. Prices and shipping costs are reasonable, and next-day delivery is available via UPS to most addresses in the United States.

Uline   www.uline.com

Like Associated Bag, Uline has a wide selection and good service. Prices and shipping costs are a bit higher.

Hillas Packaging Network www.hillas.com

Papermart www.papermart.com

Packaging Price www.packagingprice.com

Fast-Pack www.fast-pack.com

Gator Pack www.gatorpack.com

ESupplyStore www.esupplystore.com

PacnSeal www.pacnseal.com

PakOutlet www.pakoutlet.com

Reliable Office Supplies www.reliable.com

Browncor www.browncor.com

Wholesale Packaging Supply
www.wholesalepackaging.com

VeriPack www.veripack.com

Viking www.viking.com

Appendix 4
Amazon Best Practices

Listing Items and Inventory Management

☐ Update your online inventory daily to avoid stock-outs, which may occur when an Amazon buyer purchases an item from you, but you no longer have that item on hand. Making updates is especially important if the inventory you are selling on Amazon Marketplace is also for sale through other venues.

☐ Before pricing your items, research prices for comparable products on Amazon Marketplace and make adjustments if necessary.

☐ If an item has been listed for more than 30 days and has not sold, check your pricing to make sure that it is competitive and make changes if necessary.

☐ Amazon has a vacation settings feature, which removes your listings when you are not available to ship books out. This feature may take up to 36 hours to remove your listings and another 36 hours to restore them. During this period, listings cannot be modified or deleted. Read more about using this feature by visiting the Seller Account and Preferences help page.

Order Management

☐ Check your Amazon Payments Account regularly for important updates on your sales, rather than relying exclusively on e-mail notifications. You can access Payments through your Seller Account.

☐ Provide high-quality customer service, which includes handling refunds and returns in a timely manner. If you are unable to fill an order, refund it within 48 hours. Instructions are on the Refunds & Invoices page.

☐ Use the A-to-z guarantee only as a last resort when resolving matters with buyers. Multiple guarantee claims are an indication of seller performance problems.

Fulfillment

☐ Always ship your items within two business days of order notification. This is required.

☐ Include a packing slip with your item. Either cut one out from the "Sold--Ship Now" e-mail or create your own.

☐ Review the shipping and packing guidelines on Amazon's help pages carefully.

☐ Include a note with your package with your contact information and encourage your buyer to leave you feedback at www.amazon.com/feedback.

☐ Send buyers a ship confirmation e-mail after you have shipped their order, and include tracking or delivery confirmation numbers if they are available.

☐ For additional help with this topic, visit Amazon help pages, click on "Selling at Amazon.com," and

and then on the list click on "Fulfillment, Getting Paid, and Feedback."

Customer Service

☐ Answer all buyer inquiries within 24 hours of receipt. Good communication with buyers promotes good feedback for sellers.

☐ Amazon.com was founded on providing an extraordinary experience for buyers. Customers have come to expect this type of service, and that is what keeps them coming back for more purchases. As a seller, you are now in control of the same experience for your buyers: never lose sight of this philosophy.

Security

☐ Change your password regularly.

☐ Consider setting up a separate bank account for disbursements from your Amazon Payments account.

☐ Amazon.com never asks you to verify sensitive information via e-mail. Submit such information only when completing an order on Amazon's Web site, registering for Amazon Payments, or contacting Amazon directly through their Web forms.

☐ Review the terms of Amazon's online privacy notice and their other privacy and security resources.

☐ If you are ever in doubt about the authenticity of an e-mail that appears to be from Amazon, visit Amazon's site directly by typing the address into your browser bar, rather than clicking any links in the e-mail.

Source: Amazon.com

Appendix 5
More Resources

Here are some other resources you may find helpful in learning about bookselling, both in the beginning and as you advance to new levels.

Amazon Seller Discussion Board

http://forums.prosperotechnologies.com/am-sellconnect/start

Advice and discussion topics for new sellers and old pros alike. Site also contains separate boards for official Amazon announcements; listing management; shipping, feedback, and returns; and third-party services for sellers.

This discussion board is a great resource for sellers – it's like having a business consultant working for you at no charge. Any reasonable question posted on the board is likely to get a prompt response.

EBay Booksellers Discussion Board

http://forums.ebay.com/db1/forum.jspa?forumID=4

Views and advice on eBay bookselling strategies, general questions on book grading.

Book Sale Finder www.booksalefinder.com

Calendar listings of upcoming library sales and book fairs nationwide. Also operates an e-mail notification service for book sales. Classified advertisements.

Basestealer.com www.basestealer.com
Internet fraud prevention resource.

Roman Numeral and Date Conversion
www.guernsey.net/~sgibbs/roman.html

Independent Online Booksellers Association www.ioba.org
International association of independent booksellers. Advocates standards and buyer protection.

Guide to Rare and Old Book Values
www.fadedgiant.net
Auction prices for over 45,000 collectible and rare books, auction selling tips, autograph gallery, glossary, and links.

AB Bookman's Weekly
www.abbookman.com
Resources for antique, rare, and used book dealers, collectors, and buyers

Book Source Magazine
www.booksourcemagazine.com

This hard-copy monthly magazine sponsors this Web site with expanded online sections such as book search. Magazine includes auction results, book show information, editorials, opinion, features.

Firsts Magazine www.firsts.com
Book collecting, including first editions, rare, and antique books.

Antiquarian Book Fairs www.bookfairs.com
Listings of antiquarian book fairs and book print and paper shows in the United States.

Rare Book News www.rarebooknews.com
Daily news and commentary on rare books, collectors, booksellers, and librarians.

Appendix 6
Further Reading

The books listed below are widely available. You can usually find the academic works, designated with asterisks (*), online by searching for the title on Google.com.

Used Book Market Analysis. Jeff Hayes. Book Industry Study Group, InfoTrends/CAP Ventures.

* Consumer Surplus in the Digital Economy: Estimating the Value of Increased Product Variety at Online Booksellers. Erik Mrynjolfsson, Yu (Jeffrey) Hu, Michael D. Smith. Sloan School of Management, Massachusetts Institute of Technology, Cambridge, MA.

Book Finds: How to Find, Buy, and Sell Used and Rare Books. Ian C. Ellis. 2001, Perigee.

Pocket Guide to the Identification of First Editions. Bill McBride. 2001, McBride Publications.

Complete Guide to Starting a Used Bookstore: Old Books Into Gold. Dale L. Gilbert. 1986, Chicago Review Press.

Selling Used Books Online: The Complete Guide to Bookselling at Amazon's Marketplace and Other Online Sites. Stephen Windwalker. 2002, Harvard Perspectives Press.

ABCs for Book Collectors. John Carter. 2004, Oak Knoll Publishing.

The Perfect Store: Inside eBay. Adam Cohen. 2002, Back Bay Books.

* Internet Exchanges for Used Books: An Empirical Analysis of Product Cannibalization and Welfare Impact. 2005. Anidya Ghose, New York University and Rahul Telang, Carnegie Mellon University.

* Measuring Prices and Price Competition Online: Amazon and Barnes and Noble. Austan Goolsbee, Judith Chevalier. 2002, Yale International Center for Finance.

* Are Durable Goods Consumers Forward Looking? Evidence from College Textbooks. 2004, Judith A. Chevalier, Yale School of Management, Austan Goolsbee, Unversity of Chicago Graduate School of Business.

* The Management of E-Commerce Strategies for Sustaining Competitive Advantage in the Online Bookselling Industry: The Case of Amazon.com. Colin Combe. 2002, Glasgow Caledonian University.

Among the Gently Mad: Perspectives and Strategies for the Book Hunter in the 21st Century. Nicholas A. Basbanes. 2002, Henry Holt & Co.

Small Time Operator: How to Start Your Own Business, Keep Your Books, Pay your Taxes and Stay Out of Trouble. Bernard Kamoroff. 2004, Bell Springs Publishing.

Collectable Paperback Books: A New Vintage Paperback Price Reference. Jeff Canja. 2002, Glenmoor Publishing.

Appendix 7
Glossary

ABAA Antiquarian Booksellers' Association of America.

Advanced Reading Copy (ARC) A prepublication copy of the book distributed to book reviews and sellers, usually paperbound, perhaps without cover art.

Antiquarian Old or rare books that may be suitable for collecting.

ASIN (Amazon Standard Identification Number) A code used by Amazon.com to identify each product listed on its site. For books, the ASIN is usually the ISBN number (see ISBN, below), but for other products a unique ASIN is generated when the item is uploaded to the company's catalog.

Association copy A book that appears to have belonged to the author or someone closely associated with the author.

Backstrip A strip used to reinforce the back of folded sheets in the spine's binding.

Boards The front and back covers of a hardcover.

Bookplate A small paper pasted to the endpaper to indicate ownership. It sometimes reads "From the Library of _____."

Bumped Refers to a book whose cover corners or spine end has been damaged or bent because the book was dropped.

Chipped Refers to a book whose dust jacket or binding has small pieces missing, broken off.

Dog-eared Refers to pages that have been folded down at the corner and used as a placeholder by the reader.

Dust jacket or dust wrapper The outer paper folded around a hardcover binding as a protective layer.

Endpaper A sheet of paper glued to the inner covers to join the text block and case.

Ephemera Printed matter that serves as memorabilia, such as postcards, programs, pamphlets, advertising, stick stubs, playbills.

Errata A list of errors and corrections found after a book's production, usually printed on a separate sheet of paper.

Ex-library or exlib A book that has been deaccessioned from a library or collection and has some library marking.

Ex-libris A book acquired from a private library or collection instead of a public library. May indicate presence of a bookplate.

Fine A book with no defects, in brand new condition.

First edition A copy of a book that was produced during the publisher's initial printing press run.

Foxing Brown spots resembling mold along the paper edge on the top or bottom of a book, caused by age and chemical reactions.

Gilt edges Page edges that are smooth and have gold coloring or gold leaf applied.

Glassine A transparent paper dust cover.

Gutter Inside margins of two facing pages. Sometimes refers to the groove along the joint of the spine and boards.

Half leather Indicates the spine and corners are bound in leather and the other part of the binding is paper or cloth.

Highlighting Brightly colored translucent markings or underlinings produced when the reader uses a pen to mark the text.

Hinge Flexible area where book cover and spine adjoin. A worn-out book sometimes has broken or cracked hinges.

Hurt A new book that has suffered some cosmetic damage, dents or dings, during shipment from the manufacturer or from being handled in a bookstore. Usually is a perfectly usable book but not suitable for sale in a new bookstore, and is returned to the publisher.

Impression The copies of a book printed during a press run. The set of books produced during the initial press run is known as a first edition.

Inscribed Indicates a book was signed by the author, usually with a brief message to the owner of the copy.

IOBA Independent Online Booksellers Association. A trade association of online booksellers.

ISBN (International Standard Book Number) A series of ten digits used, along with a corresponding bar code, to identify a book or a certain edition of a book. Older books won't have a bar code; look inside the cover for an ISBN. On some books printed in the 1970s, you'll see a 9-digit "Standard Book Number," which you can convert into an ISBN by adding a leading zero. Earlier books don't have ISBNs. Because the ISBN system is running out of 10-digit numbers, ISBNs will be expanded to 13 digits beginning in 2007.

Limited edition The book is one of a small number of copies printed at one time. May be numbered, for example, 120/300, meaning number 120 out of an edition of 300.

Marginalia Notes written in the page margins around the text.

Mass-market paperback Standard sized small paperbacks, about four inches wide and seven inches tall, also known as pocket books.

Mint copy A perfect copy of a book that has the same appearance as it did the day it was produced.

Modern first edition A first edition of a book published within the past century.

Out of print No longer carried by the publisher. No new copies are produced for sale.

Presentation copy A book given by the author to an acquaintance, usually with an inscription indicating this.

Price clipped The original list price has been snipped with scissors from the corner of the dust jacket.

Reading copy A worn copy of a book suitable for reading but not in acceptable condition for collectors.

Remainder Books returned to the publisher unsold are "remaindered" and sold off cheaply to make room for new books. Often the publisher will mark the bottom of the books with a black marker; this "remainder mark" indicates that the copy can't be returned for a refund of the retail price.

Shelf wear Wear around the edges of a book from being handled and rubbing against other surfaces on a bookshelf.

Signed A book that contains the author's signature only, no other text.

Spine – A book's back, on which the title usually appears. It is covered with the backstrip.

SKU – (Stock keeping unit) -- A unique numeric identifier, usually maintained in a database, to designate an item in inventory.

Trade paperback A paperback book larger in size than a mass-market paperback; it may be the same size as a hardcover.

Uncorrected proof A pre-publication copy of the book used during the editing or proofreading process or distributed to book reviewers.

9 780977 240609